VIEW

from the

ALTAR

VIEW

from the

ALTAR

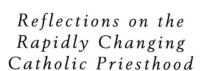

*Reflections on the
Rapidly Changing
Catholic Priesthood*

HOWARD P. BLEICHNER, S.S.

A Crossroad Book
The Crossroad Publishing Company
New York

*54989961

The Crossroad Publishing Company
16 Penn Plaza, 481 Eighth Avenue
New York, NY 10001

Copyright © 2004 by Howard P. Bleichner, S.S.

The Scripture quotations contained herein are from the New Revised Standard Version Bible, copyright © 1993 by the Division of Christian Education of the National Council of the Churches of Christ in the U.S.A. Used by permission. All rights reserved.

Printed in the United States of America

Library of Congress Cataloging-in-Publication Data

Bleichner, Howard P.
    View from the altar : reflections on the changing Catholic priesthood / Howard Bleichner
        p. cm.
    Includes bibliographical references and index.
    ISBN 0-8245-2141-2 (alk. paper)
    1. Priesthood. 2. Catholic Church – Clergy.   I. Title.
    BX1912.B595 2004
    262'.142 – dc22

                                                        2004007976

1 2 3 4 5 6 7 8 9 10   10 09 08 07 06 05 04

To Family and Friends
in Remembrance and Gratitude

CONTENTS

ACKNOWLEDGMENTS

THIS BOOK WAS WRITTEN while I was on sabbatical after a ten-year stint in administration and teaching at the Theological College of the Catholic University of America. It is the fruit as well of more than thirty years in seminary formation. I wish to acknowledge the help of many friends and colleagues: Monsignor J. Patrick Browne, Sister Barbara Carroll, S.N.J.M., Fathers Timothy Cusick, S.S., Clement Gardner, Thomas Hurst, S.S., Robert F. Leavitt, S.S., Kenan Osborne, O.F.M., Kevin Seasoltz, O.S.B., Ronald Witherup, S.S., and John Jones at the Crossroad Publishing Company. Their comments and criticism were invariably helpful. The emphases and errors of the book are my own.

Introduction

HOPE IN A STORM-TOSSED SEA

T HIS BOOK on priestly formation and priestly spirituality was begun a year after the tragedy of September 11, 2001, and nine months after the sex abuse scandals in the Roman Catholic Church began to unfold. Since it was written and will be read in the continuing light of those events, a word on each seems appropriate, indeed unavoidable.

It is sometimes said that no century, much less a millennium, ever began on its first day or in its first year. The twentieth century began in 1914 with the outbreak of World War I, just as the century before it began with the final defeat of Napoleon in 1815.[1] Our new century did not begin on January 1, 2000, but on September 11, 2001, because this is the day the shape of the future first became clear.

With the destruction of the Twin Towers in New York City, a long war has opened that will irrevocably mark the future, a war between civilization as we have known it and the terrorism of individuals and small groups as we are beginning to know it. In this war, the difference between domestic and foreign terrorism is sometimes small. Prior to 9/11 the familiar brands of terrorism were street crime and school violence, with teenagers down the block armed or making bombs in the basement or garage. It is fair to say that the attack on the Twin Towers from without struck deeply resonant chords within a society already primed for violence. In effect, 9/11 has ushered in a harsher social climate that will define the foreseeable future in every way.

It did not take long for the bitter winds to hit the Catholic Church. Just five months after 9/11, beginning in January 2002, the Archdiocese of Boston became the epicenter of sexual abuse scandals that spread across the United States. Former priests

John J. Geoghan and Paul R. Shanley and then Archbishop Bernard Cardinal Law of Boston lent faces to the story. Cases of sexual misconduct going back fifty years were resurrected. Earlier settlements by church officials were also reexamined. A pattern seemed to emerge: abuse by priests, coverup by bishops, cash-for-silence settlements by lawyers — even, it was alleged, the intimidation of public officials by a powerful and influential institution to shield the church's reputation at all cost. As old cases were brought back to life, they spilled over into the present. Since it was impossible to say the old pattern had stopped, it also became difficult to distinguish today's priests from their predecessors. A cloud of suspicion descended on all priests.

The storm picked up additional force as it moved through *old* troubled waters. Lingering fissures between Catholic liberals and conservatives reopened, providing a lens to read the situation and diagnose the problem. To neoconservatives, the scandals revealed the church's departure from orthodox belief and practice. The solution, according to Father John Neuhaus, was "fidelity, fidelity, fidelity." No more nods and winks to priestly misconduct on the part of bishops. Liberal voices concluded that mandatory celibacy and the church's refusal to ordain married men and women were the reason for the sad state of the clergy and indicated the obvious way out of the impasse. Both sides saw a reflection of their own image in the scandals. In that sense, neither had much new or enlightening to say. Cross breezes struck the situation from another quarter. Just as revelation of priestly abuse and episcopal complicity were appearing, oddly symmetrical scandals, as if on cue, roiled the corporate world at its highest levels, with the collapse of Enron, WorldCom, and Arthur Andersen. Especially troubling were the revelations of "irregular accounting procedures," cooking the books.

Priestly misconduct was joined to these corporate scandals by two common features: predatory behavior and lack of accountability. Public suspicion of large institutions and insider chicanery was reinforced from another side.

By any measure, the sexual abuse scandals have struck the Catholic Church in the United States with the force of a tsunami, dealing the Catholic priesthood the worst blow in memory. Before our eyes, the reputation of the Roman Catholic priesthood experienced a slow-motion implosion. In only six months, the priesthood seemed to melt from a widely respected vocation to a suspect calling, tarnished by a broad-based suspicion of child abuse and populated largely by gay men. In January 2002, it was a cause for pride to wear a Roman collar; by June, it had become an embarrassment.

Much as 9/11 reveals the face of the foreseeable future for the country, so too the sex abuse scandals define the challenge facing the American Catholic Church in general and the priesthood in particular. Genuine solutions still seem distant. Quick answers after the fact often resembled extensions of the problem, panicky moves to staunch the flow of blood and head off the crisis. The first draft of "The Charter for the Protection of Children and Young People" prepared by the U.S. Conference of Catholic Bishops in June 2002 was a case in point. The Charter seemed in equal measure solution and symptom. Anxious to reassure a nervous public, it slighted the rights of priests in various ways, yet passed mildly over the topic of episcopal complicity. But the early discussion had the merit of contributing a watchword to the situation, "zero tolerance": zero tolerance on sex abuse, on complicity in sex abuse, on lack of accountability, on poorly run parishes and mismanaged dioceses. Like Ockham's razor, zero tolerance cuts through abuse and obfuscation, opening a broadly unfolding process of reform that must run its course. But it is naive to think that the sexual abuse scandals move at their own pace, somehow on autopilot. If the church lost control of the situation, others have filled the vacuum. If Daniel Lyons writing in *Forbes* is right, genuine victims mix with doubtful ones in a train steered by high-profile lawyers, operating on a finely honed formula, toward a goal of five billion dollars in compensation.[2]

What is clear now is the *magnitude* of the problem. Inside the church, the scandals have opened a series of hairline fractures that could grow larger. Publicly, the Holy See objected to features of the draft Charter that ran counter to canon law and church practice. Privately, more than one Vatican source wondered if the American bishops had lost their bearings, if not their nerve. While reassuring Catholics about the safety of their children, the bishops opened a potentially significant rift with priests. Numerous cracks have also opened between laity and clergy. Are children safe with priests, and can bishops be trusted to supervise the priests? By any measure, the Catholic laity seem on the verge of a major upgrade in their responsibilities within the church. Increasingly, lay Catholics are called to verify new and stricter standards of priestly conduct and episcopal accountability. It remains to be seen how much the scandals will erode Catholic practice.[3]

While the scandals have had a fracturing effect within the church, they seem to have crystallized public opinion in the larger society. The church's positions on family, sexuality, celibacy, abortion, capital punishment, the ordination of women, and social justice have always been countercultural in different ways and were greeted with varying degrees of opposition in society. But like it or not, priestly celibacy is the usual billboard on which the church's integrity is displayed. Now the *personal* lapses of priests and bishops seemed to undermine the church's *public* credibility. For that reason, the church's voice in the public forum has grown more quiet. No one wants to hear large pronouncements from a church whose own house is in disorder.

A storm-tossed sea may not seem the ideal setting for an essay on priestly formation and priestly spirituality. But it takes only a moment to realize that genuine spiritualities are seldom the product of calm waters or the fruit of armchair musings. On the contrary, they grow in times when good people have their backs to the wall and must reach deep within themselves as the outside scenery remains bleak. Recall that Ezekiel's great sermon on hope was delivered to a field of dry bones. In this sense, the crisis facing the priesthood will be resolved only by a spiritual response. The indictments are far too serious to be met on an intermediate level, e.g., more psychotherapy for troubled priests. Indeed, if this is not precisely the moment for a reflection on priestly spirituality, then I am sorely mistaken in my instincts. In his apostolic letter *Novo Millennio Ineunte* (2001), Pope John Paul II begins with Jesus's invitation to his disciples to "put out into the deep" for a catch. *Duc in altum* (Luke 5:4). "These words ring out for us today, and they invite us to remember the past with gratitude, to live the present with enthusiasm, and to look forward to the future with confidence."[4]

The invitation to put out into the deep in a storm-tossed sea may seem counterintuitive. But since John Paul II was elected in 1978, a single phrase has marked his pontificate. We heard it in his first homily in St. Peter's square in 1978, and he has repeated it again and again for twenty-six years. These were words from Christ to Peter in troubled waters, repeated often in the Gospels, words "not spoken into a void," John Paul later wrote, but spoken to each one of us: *be not afraid.*[5] In troubled waters, when the future ahead is unclear and danger surely lurks — then, above all, be not afraid. Christ the Lord is with us. Deep water for a good catch, symbol of the church's mission, is also the place where an anchor can hold, symbol of Christ's presence. Such a setting is where spirituality begins. The image catches the overarching goal of this essay: to offer hope about the future of the priesthood.

The present situation determines the approach, the challenge, and the purpose of an essay like this. Because of the rapidity of the onset and development of the crisis, some historical context is needed. At minimum, the melt-down of a an honored institution needs to be surrounded by fifty years of history. A context will also provide the rudiments of an interpretation. Priestly spirituality flows from the gift of the sacrament of Holy Orders and the personal contribution of each individual candidate. Those two sides constitute the heart of the endeavor that follows.

The challenge facing an essay on priestly spirituality at this time is to stay on focus. Acknowledging the seriousness of the current scandals at full strength risks having them monopolize the discussion. Ultimately, this essay is not about priestly misconduct but about priestly spirituality in an ancient and honored vocation that finds itself at a critical moment. But without a credible interpretation of recent events, the road to the main topic is blocked. And we should not fool ourselves here. It will take a hard-fought battle through difficult terrain to reach an upland where we can credibly turn to the subject of priestly formation and priestly spirituality.

At this critical point, however, I would like to go back to basics and talk about essential elements of priestly life. John Lukacs makes a helpful distinction between motives and purposes. "Motives come from the past; purposes involve the pull of the future."[6] There is motivation enough from the past for priests to struggle through the current crisis. But will they ever be successful without a sense of higher purpose that pulls them into the future? I think not, and therefore I hope to make a contribution on the latter score. Priests not only need to take themselves seriously in terms of the highest ideals of their vocation; they also need to recall the corporate challenge, larger than the present crisis, to carry the mandate of Vatican Council II into the third generation of its reception.

View from the Altar is for seminarians, priests, and bishops, but also for a wider audience of Catholics now more interested in how priests are formed. They also wish to make sense of the sexual abuse scandals that have struck the Catholic Church. Everyone wants to place them in a context that answers the question why they happened when they happened. *View from the Altar* is also an essay on spirituality. Spirituality is not confined to a clerical enclave. There is much on prayer and the evangelical counsels that pertains first to Christian living and then focuses on those in formation for the priesthood and those ordained.

Few people can claim objectivity about the priesthood, and my opinions, points of view, prejudices, and limitations will soon become clear. In lieu of a claim to objectivity, I will fly my own colors clearly. I am a Sulpician priest, ordained in 1967 for the diocese of Pittsburgh with a doctorate from the University of Tübingen (1973). My own involvement in priestly formation has been in seminaries in Baltimore, San Francisco, and Washington, D.C. I have been up to my ears in priestly formation since Vatican II. I do not represent an outside voice — quite the opposite. I do hope, however, to claim a certain independence of mind.

PART ONE

THE SITUATION

Chapter One

THE SCANDALS

T O INTERPRET the recent sexual abuse scandals in the Catholic priesthood, it is important to place the narrow slice of time of January–June 2002 against the backdrop of the church's life from 1950 to the present — the years just before the Second Vatican Council, which took place in 1962–65, down to the turn of the millennium.

A phenomenon one observes among young Catholics, especially seminarians, pinpoints the challenge. As they become more involved in the church's life, young Catholics often resemble theatergoers who enter a play late in the second act with only a limited sense of the larger plot that preceded their arrival. In truth, they are strangers to the drama they are watching, a drama in which they may later be appearing in feature roles. The transition between generations always resembles different acts in the same play. When an event as unique as Vatican II punctuates the action, the differences become all the greater. The scandals only raise the stakes again. Therefore the reasons for a narrative of events as close to lived experience as possible grow all the more compelling, not least of all because our goal here is not finally to make sense out of bad theology but of bad behavior (though the two may be related). For many reasons a portrait of the past, as life-sized as possible, is called for to place the scandals in a context that may illumine them.

Such desires dictate the approach. I am looking for a "thick" description of the recent past, in Clifford Geertz's phrase,[1] still closer to Avishai Margalit's use of the term.[2] By any measure, the shift to Vatican II's understanding of the church, while continuous with the past, was also revolutionary, like water that becomes colder and colder, then suddenly ceases to be a liquid at all. The same analogy could be applied to the priesthood. This approach seeks to capture the scope of such vast changes by accumulating a series of small examples — images, tableaux, practices — that presage the appearance of something new. It will advance an argument as it seeks to illumine key turning points in a fast-paced story. In regard to the latter, concrete examples have a way of bringing the past back to life that escapes the purview of formal analysis. Hence while the chapter will present an interpretation of recent events, it will resemble as well the sketch of a portrait of the priesthood over two generations.

Just as an archeologist collects innumerable shards of pottery and other artifacts in order to finally create a fresher, more concrete image of the past, I hope in this way to remain as close to lived experience as possible. The focus will be placed squarely on the Eucharist and the sacrament of Penance from before Vatican II down to the present. Codifying the medieval tradition, the Council of Trent (1545–63) defined the priesthood in terms of these two sacraments: "the power to consecrate and the power to forgive sins."[3] These powers are unique to priestly ministry — what the priest and no one else can do. My assumption is that if we follow the changes in these sacraments, the lived experience of priests in the last two generations will come to life at its most vivid and characteristic points.

THE EUCHARIST

Before the Council

In the 1950s, children were closely instructed on how to receive Holy Communion: hands steepled, tongues extended, eyes closed, with the clear admonition, *"Don't* chew the host. Let it dissolve on your tongue." The pure white hosts used at mass looked more like food from heaven than earthly bread. And so the hosts were treated. In some Irish-American families, it was the custom to drink a glass of water at home after communion to ensure that all remnants of the consecrated host were washed down before breakfast. And no one, *no one*, touched a consecrated host, except a priest or a deacon.

Holy Communion was received *kneeling* at the communion rail under *one species*, a single white host. Each of these practices represented a victory in old battles. The first — what the Book of Common Prayer called the "Black Rubric," that is, the reception of communion kneeling — was distinctive to Catholics and High Anglicans. It was a special mark of respect for the real presence of Christ in the Eucharist. The second — reception under one species only — was against the Utraquists, followers of John Huss (1369–1415), who asserted that the people should receive communion under both species, just as the priest does. No, said the Council of Trent, the whole Christ — Body, Blood, Soul, and Divinity — is contained in every particle of the Eucharist.

The communion rail itself constituted a statement. It marked off the "sacred space" from which the laity were excluded, with rare exceptions. It was rumored that a mitered abbess might enter to sing the epistle. Normally, women entered the sanctuary only for their marriage and their funeral. Still visible in many churches, the main altar itself made a further statement. Three steps separated the high altar from the floor of the sanctuary — the top step for the priest, the second for the deacon, the third for the subdeacon. The three-step arrangement enshrined the paradigm form of the old mass, the solemn high mass, in its most dramatic form, the pontifical solemn high mass in one of its variations: the bishop off to the side in choir robes, his vestments carefully arranged on the main altar before the tabernacle. The vestments were brought down to him one by one by the master of ceremonies as he quietly recited the vesting prayers. It was like the dressing of a monarch, a private affair become public ceremony.

A deacon's hands trembled the first time he gave out communion. Indeed, the distribution of communion itself was a complicated affair. The priest made the sign of the cross with the consecrated host before each communicant, reciting each time, "Corpus Domini nostri Jesu Christi custodiat animam tuam in vitam eternam" (May the body of our Lord Jesus Christ keep your soul unto eternal life). After the consecration, the thumb and first finger of the priest were joined together until the final ablution to ensure that the smallest particle of the host not be dropped. The node on the stem of old chalices was so fashioned that they could be more easily grasped with joined fingers. In the 1950s, the number of communicants in a packed church amounted to only a few rows at the communion rail. Older and younger people predominated. Two or at most three priests could distribute communion at even the most crowded masses. Many Catholics attended mass regularly but never went to communion. One learned not to ask why.

The priest was the single, sole minister of the mass whose action mattered. If the epistle was read in English by a layperson, it was simultaneously recited in Latin by the priest at the altar. So, too, all other parts of the mass that were sung or read by others: they acquired validity only when the priest said them. The centrality of the priest at the Eucharist to the exclusion of other ministers is a vivid witness to the way in which the priesthood had literally swallowed up all other liturgical ministries in the church. (By way of exception, Pius X stated that those who sang at mass discharged an authentic liturgical office. Since women were therefore automatically excluded from singing, this meant that officially women were prohibited from belonging to church choirs until 1958, when the situation was rectified.)[4] The only other voice at the liturgy was the youthful piping of the server, called in Italian *chierichetti,* little clerics, minipriests. Although these restrictions on participation had begun to change with the introduction of the dialogue mass, officially they remained until 1964. Mass was a priestly activity that the faithful attended and followed, but they did not take part more formally in it.

THE EUCHARIST BEFORE VATICAN II

The setting: a packed church in summer in the 1950s before air conditioning. Preaching was suspended for the summer months (which few Catholics counted a loss). The liturgy of the Word did not belong to the "three principal parts of the mass" — offertory, consecration, and communion — required for valid attendance. Two giant fans were placed in the sanctuary, facing the congregation. A visiting priest, not conversant with the setup, stepped in front of one of these fans with a ciborium, brimming with consecrated hosts. A blast of air hit it and sent a shower of thirty or forty hosts soaring out into the congregation, depositing them like unwanted manna on the occupants of the first pews who sat transfixed as the hosts descended. They knew better than to pick them up or even touch them. One woman had a special look of consternation on her face as she realized that a host was descending in her direction, finally coming to rest in the veil of her hat.

The priest sent the servers back to the sacristy for thirty or forty purificators and finger towels and went about picking the hosts off people and from the floor, placing a purificator where each one had fallen. People tiptoed around these cloths when they left. The priest returned after mass to wash each place where a sacred host had dropped.

Typical of the church before the council, the incident illustrates the enormous fear and trembling that surrounded the Eucharist for Catholics, a *Mysterium tremendum et fascinans.* Most lay people would have hesitated to approach the tabernacle too closely. But the priest — he could change bread and wine into the Body and Blood of Christ and could touch the sacred host with impunity. He was himself a hallowed person.

Not surprisingly, this sharp and tangible sense of sacred space and sacred presence at the Eucharist was linked to a series of *internal* attitudes outside the mass. These comprised a circle of taboos that surrounded priestly life and held it in place. Every priest, for example, was obliged under the pain of mortal sin to recite the entire breviary daily. It mattered little how much he understood as long as the obligation was completed. The sense of taboo was even more graphically displayed when priests had difficulty reciting the Words of Institution. If priests were the sole active ministers of the Eucharist, their own activity was condensed into the climactic Words of Institution, the handful of words that brought Christ down into the bread and wine on the altar. It was agonizing to watch a scrupulous priest attempt to get through the words of consecration, the first words "Hoc est enim..." repeated over and over again as he struggled to recite the formula.

Such attitudes and practices were woven into the fabric of priestly life. The strictures were seldom explained and rarely taught. They were learned by watching and imitation, the way taboos are transmitted. Indeed, the silence that surrounded them was a sign of their self-evident potency. They were further mirrored in *social* attitudes in the Catholic community, emerging now from its immigrant roots. A series of taboos regulated priestly conduct in society, especially in regard to sexuality. They applied to Catholic life in general but reached a special intensity regarding priests. The priest was always called "Father"; in effect, he was never out of his role. These were barriers against certain activities, not reasoned, moral limits that a person consciously adopted, but rather viscerally understood taboos that, if broken, could call down thunderbolts from on high, prohibitions endowed with numinous power at every point, not unlike the host at mass.

Vatican II

The Second Vatican Council introduced changes in the liturgy, especially the Eucharist. In a symbolic medium like the liturgy, small, seemingly incidental changes are often endowed with enormous significance far beyond their doctrinal content. Indeed, minor and major changes are often indistinguishable at first glance. With the stroke of a pen in 1910, for example, Pius X lowered the age for First Holy Communion to age seven. Suddenly, an entire culture sprang up around the practice: young girls in white dresses and white veils with white prayer books and little boys in their first pair of long pants with black prayer books.[5] This type of change was a precursor of Vatican II.

The Second Vatican Council approved the Constitution on the Sacred Liturgy by a vote of 2147 in favor, 4 opposed on December 3, 1963, the four hundredth anniversary of the close of the Council of Trent. The Constitution was scheduled to go into effect on February 16, 1964.[6] It is accurate to regard the Constitution as a series of master directives for the overhaul of the entire Catholic liturgy. The date of implementation marked the beginning of the process. The task was completed in a little more than a decade. Many of the most significant changes — the use of the vernacular, communion under both kinds, concelebration — were consciously introduced through loophole clauses. These constituted strategic breeches in a dam that was quickly swept away. Once set in motion, the reform of the liturgy took on its own momentum, like a vast tide that might be channeled but could not be stopped until it reached equilibrium. The council fathers could hardly have foreseen what they had set in motion on December 3, 1964.

In this vast shift, two elements stand out as symbolic statements of the new liturgy and hallmarks of the new era. First, the vernacular in the mass and the divine office quickly moved from exception to rule. Second, the turning of the altars — mass facing the people — became the special tone-setter of the new Eucharist. The priest (soon to be termed the "presider" in official documents) was not only to *say* but to *pray* the mass. One after another, the old lines of sacred demarcation fell. Catholics began to receive communion standing and under both species. In 1969, communion in the hand was permitted, followed shortly by the introduction of extraordinary ministers of the Eucharist. The priest was no longer directed to hold thumb and forefinger together after the consecration. Communion rails were removed. The tabernacle was moved from the main altar to a side altar or special chapel. The "feel" of Catholic churches changed dramatically. Catholic church architecture was traditionally designed to draw the eye to the tabernacle, the focus of attention. Now the focus shifted to the altar of sacrifice, to the "action" of the eucharistic banquet rather than the "static" presence of the reserved sacrament.

By any measure, the council had introduced a vast revolution in the practice and sensibility surrounding the Eucharist. If a single phrase can capture it, the "democratization of the Eucharist" comes close. Christ's gift of the Eucharist belongs to the whole church, and it should be made as inviting and as accessible as possible. Likewise, the celebration of the Eucharist should involve the whole church. As we look back on this revolution after almost two generations, two features stand out. First, it is amazing how much the reforms of the Eucharist got right on the first go-round. Second, it will take the lived experience of several generations before the new liturgy fully settles into place. It needs to grow its own moss on its sides, to develop its own forms of devotional life, and that process takes time. The first impact of the liturgical reforms on traditional

Catholic devotion was largely disparaging. Only a few traditional practices — rosary, stations of the cross — made it through the fire relatively unscathed.

A NEW STYLE OF CATHOLIC COMMUNICANT

Catholics used to approach the communion rail like the young St. Alphonsus, hands folded, eyes cast up or down, the host reverently received on the tongue, slowly dissolving in the mouth. Quickly this changed. Liturgy watchers noted that the papal masters of ceremony — long arbiters of custom — no longer steepled their hands. They cupped their palms. Others followed suit. Still others swung their arms at their side as they marched up to communion, a hymn book clutched in one hand. A new style of communicant was born.

If one image caught these changes, it was that of a single seminarian, clad in open clerical shirt, jeans, and sandals, striding up to receive communion. He looked the priest squarely in the eye, responding to the words, "Body of Christ" with a resounding "Amen." On receiving the sacred host, he began to visibly chew it. He was followed by a long line of seminarians who approached the Eucharist in just the same way. They seldom missed a verse of the hymn they were singing as they came up to communion. "Here we are all together as we sing this song merrily, here we are as we sing our praise to Thee." In a scant two or three years, Gregorian chant had been replaced by English hymns that often had the same charm as commercial jingles in the 1960s. "Good Lord," an old priest dolefully observed, "here comes the future."

There were reactions, casualties in the war, those whose memory of the old liturgy did not go quietly into the night. The point of no return for Father Frederick Schell, S.J., came in 1977. "They told me I would have to give out communion in the hand on November 20, 1977. I told people at the time, 'This is a sacrilege. They can't make me do it.' So I preached against it on November 13, 1977, and by the next week I was gone."[7] But these were exceptions. The new liturgy was generally greeted with infectious enthusiasm. Most Catholics did not compare new to old. They liked the old liturgy. They just liked the new liturgy more.

Vatican II started a revolution in the practice of the Eucharist that hit the Catholic Church as a whole and struck the priesthood dead center.

THE SACRAMENT OF PENANCE

The fate of the two sacraments so intimately linked to the priesthood — the Eucharist and Penance — could not have been more different after the council. A striking feature of postconciliar church life was the dramatic way in which the number of communicants *rose* as the number of those who went to confession *dwindled*. What happened to the sacrament of Penance? And what happened to the priesthood so closely linked to the fate of this sacrament?

Before the Council

The later turn of events could hardly have been predicted from the regular practice of confession in the church before the council. The Council of Trent had laid the doctrinal foundation. Penitents brought their contribution, contrition, confession of sins, and the willingness to make satisfaction; all mortal sins were to be confessed in number and species. In Christ's name, the priest gave absolution. Together, these constituted the matter and form of the sacrament of Penance. Against the Synod of Pistoia (1786), Pius VI continued to encourage the confession of venial sins.[8] In exhorting the faithful to frequent devotional confession, Pius XII's encyclicals *Mystici Corporis* (1943) and *Mediator Dei* (1947) endorsed what had become standard practice across the Catholic world.

Steady and consistent teaching and exhortation over four centuries had given birth to steady and consistent practice that could be observed in almost every Catholic parish before the council. Children received detailed instruction about the sacrament, from the opening salutation "Bless me, Father, for I have sinned, my last confession was three weeks ago" to the "Act of Contrition," carefully memorized. A fair gauge of the practice is the fact that in a large city parish, three or four priests were fully engaged hearing confessions for an hour on Saturday afternoon and an hour on Saturday evening.

If there was a discrepancy between Catholics who went to mass and those who received communion, the gap was larger between the Catholics who went to confession and those who did not. The reasons for the latter often came down to matters like an unresolved marital situation, a sin too embarrassing to confess (usually sexual), or a bad experience with a priest in a prior confession. What people confessed was varied yet stylized. But the heart of the matter — what Catholics commonly confessed as mortal sin — usually involved only a few actions: missing mass on Sunday, eating meat on Friday, and almost everything regarding sex. These were the anchors of the sacrament of Penance in Catholic consciousness.

It was longstanding Catholic teaching that all sins against the sixth commandment were grave matter for confession. In other words, with rare exceptions all sexual sins were "objectively" mortal. Naturally, "subjective" circumstances could mitigate culpability in significant ways, but that did not alter the objective nature of the action. The irony of this teaching was not lost on Catholics. If all sexual sins were in the same category, then why be hung for a lesser offense? Why ride on the merry-go-round when the roller coaster came for the same price of admission? The law of unintended consequences was everywhere present in this teaching.

Even more to the point, the sacrament of Penance was built on a theory of sin that may not have been elegant, but was simple and straightforward. For the practice of confession to emerge and stabilize with such consistency across the Catholic world, there had to be a simple "take" on the nature of sin, available to every Catholic. And so there was. Certain actions were *objectively* wrong, and they fell into the categories of venial or mortal sins. *Subjective* circumstances could convert a serious sin into a lesser offense, culpability determined case by case.

Instruction given to seminarians about hearing confessions was not detailed. The 1983 Code of Canon Law devotes a series of canons to the minister of the sacrament (canons 965–86.)[9] Canon 979 counsels prudence and discretion in posing questions. But in practice, unwritten rules of discretionary conduct were handed down from one generation of priest to the next. The penitent accuses himself or herself. The priest was to regard himself largely as the silent recipient of confession. The best confessors gave wise, terse counsel, and they carefully controlled their own reactions. They themselves had heard too often of the irreparable damage inflicted by a priest's angry outburst in the confessional. When in doubt, they remained silent. There was a considerable art to hearing confessions. Reputed to have spent sixteen to eighteen hours a day in the confessional, the Cure d'Ars (1786–1859) was given as a role model to diocesan priests because he exemplified not simply patience but this special skill of hearing confessions.

CONFESSION

Hearing confessions was often like fishing — slow and routine, a matter of waiting. Catholics package their sins the same way: venial sins come first (missed morning/evening prayer), then mortal sins (stealing, fornication, adultery). The heart of the matter usually is mentioned last.

From time to time, there are startling revelations. An old pastor seeks a young priest to hear his confession. He visited a prostitute on vacation (a vacation from his vocation as well). He thinks a young priest will be so surprised he will let him off with a light penance and no lecture. He is right.

A man returns to the sacrament after fifteen years. Fifteen years ago he pressured a woman to have an abortion. He knew this was wrong. Now he wants to turn his life around, and that means confessing this sin. By the sound of the man's voice, it is clearer to the priest than to the penitent that his resolve will stick. The grace of conversion, given long ago by the risen Christ, is as palpable at that moment as on the day of the Lord's resurrection. A good confessor knows to get out of the way. The penitent's sorrow and God's forgiveness are the chief actors in the sacrament of Penance.

Why did confessions dwindle at a time when Catholic renewal was flourishing on so many levels? The fate of the sacrament is inseparable from the fate of the priesthood. What did the decline in the practice of confession portend for the priesthood?

After the Council

The factors that undermined the practice of confession pertained less to the sacrament than to its underpinnings in Catholic consciousness.

By any measure, the controversy around *Humanae Vitae* (1968), the encyclical that upheld the church's opposition to artificial contraception, holds pride of place because it affected church life so deeply on so many levels. Heretofore, conscientious Catholics did not practice birth control or, if they did, they confessed it as a sin. They did not know the church's position *could* change. Then to learn that Pope Paul VI had acted against the recommendation of his own blue-ribbon panel (and against the committee of cardinals on the panel) was not simply bewildering but broadly alienating.[10] The tepid endorsement of the papal teaching by the world's episcopal conferences carried its own message. Clergy protested. In Washington, D.C., in October 1968 Cardinal O'Boyle censured thirty-nine priests because of their vocal opposition to *Humanae Vitae*.[11] These events delivered an indirect but clear signal to the average Catholic to ignore the papal ban on birth control. This quickly became part of a larger emerging pattern. Not only did Catholics go their own way on birth control but on other medical-moral matters, including vasectomies and *in vitro* fertilization. Abortion remained the sole issue on which the church's voice was taken seriously.

The effect of this controversy on priests was enormous. Most bishops avoided Cardinal O'Boyle's path of confrontation. They were content with silent compliance on the part of priests. But many priests, younger priests especially, were as little persuaded by the encyclical's arguments as were their flock. The more thoughtful ones knew that the authority of church teaching does not stand on the reasons presented in a document. But this was not much consolation. For many priests, *Humanae Vitae* marked a watershed moment in regard to the reforms of Vatican II, soon to be followed by a mood of disillusionment. This was a sad but perhaps inevitable circumstance. The expectations that Vatican II had awakened were so high that nothing short of celestial intervention could have satisfied them.

In effect, disillusionment on birth control was a harbinger of the future. It was surely a factor propelling many idealistic young priests to leave the priesthood. When it became clear as well that the church's position on celibacy would not change, priests decamped in droves. And these were some of the best. To those who remained, an element of mild duplicity — the beginnings of what some call the "winky winky" culture — entered the picture. It was clear to bishops that large numbers of priests disagreed with the ban on birth control. It was clear to lay Catholics that bishops had no choice but to tolerate their disagreement. Who knows what the bishops themselves thought? The first of a number of elephants had entered the drawing room, large unmentionable issues that subtly dominated the scene.

The birth control controversy was complicated by developments in moral theology. Catholic moral theology was attempting to rethink its basic categories. Newer approaches like "fundamental option," "proportionalism," and "consequentialism" sprang up. They suggested different ways to calculate sin and moral responsibility. These theories seemed to speak more directly to the age than the older distinction between *objective* evil and *subjective* culpability. In one sense, these debates were arcane and not well known beyond the walls of seminaries and theological schools. In another, they were not arcane at all: they clashed directly with the birth control encyclical. Accordingly, a large and respectable wing of Catholic moral theology balked at the papal ban. After all, theologians had been right in the past when the official church teaching had been wrong. Had not the Vatican Council itself vindicated the prophetic voice of theologians more than once? Perhaps this would be the case once again.

For a generation after the council, the Catholic Church spoke with two voices on moral issues. There was the voice of Rome and the bishops, traditional positions articulated in older categories. Then there were the voices of Catholic moral theologians,

often in tenured positions at universities, who espoused more liberal positions not only on birth control but on a variety of related
topics. Newer categories, they argued, allowed for greater flexibility on masturbation, homosexuality, premarital sex, and other
sexual issues.

None of the newer theories had the effect of simplifying complex
questions. To the contrary, newer developments had the cumulative
effect of making younger priests unsure about their own thinking. What is a sin? What is a serious sin? What is a mortal sin?
What was crystal clear a generation before now became murky. The
fallout of this confusion spread in all directions. Certainly priests
seldom preached on the sacrament of Penance, no longer able to
urge Catholics to go to confession with the same conviction as
before.

In truth, the newer approaches in moral theology struck at the
foundation of the traditional practice of confession. The "action
theory" of morality — the idea that certain actions are wrong in
themselves — was not just one theory among others. It was woven
into the fabric of the sacrament. Not surprisingly, John Paul II
would base his arguments in his encyclicals *Veritatis Splendor*
(1993) and *Evangelium Vitae* (1995) on this assumption. But for
the moment, the average Catholic sensed confusion. It was hard
to avoid the impression that the sacrament of Penance was under
construction or closed for repairs.

The birth control controversy and the new developments in
Catholic moral theology took place in a wider culture that also was
in the throes of a revolution in sexual mores. The church's faltering
stand on birth control fit hand-in-glove with a new set of permissive attitudes on sexuality sweeping the country. In this climate,
when moral theologians tried to add shading to traditional Catholic positions on sexuality, the result was not greater nuance. Rather,
older positions were swept away like sand castles in a riptide and
replaced by nothing at all. Catholics began to act like everyone else
not only in regard to birth control but also in regard to premarital
sex and other sexual behavior. Once again, the church had come, if
not to accept, then at least to tolerate such developments. The effect on the practice of confession was also clear. If a sizable portion

of confessions had been devoted to sexuality, this bulwark item now slipped below the surface in the new sea of toleration. As Catholics passed into mainstream American culture, they seemed to be given a free pass on what had formerly been a central concern of confession. The church looked like a bystander to the transaction.

But it was not just a matter of old barriers falling. Catholics were deeply attracted to the humanistic psychology of Carl Rogers, Abraham Maslow, and others as a new form of spirituality. Humanistic psychology offered an alternate path between Freudian psychology and the behaviorism of B. F. Skinner. Traditional Catholic spirituality foundered on the sharp separation between nature and grace. God's grace seemed to descend vertically without discernable emotional impact, human feeling virtually excluded from the encounter. Now, by contrast, the model of self-actualizing human growth seemed to offer middle ground, a bridge from human to spiritual growth. If grace builds upon nature, so a fully actualized person seemed to represent the best candidate for growth in Christian virtue.

Humanistic psychology also offered a method. First, individuals were counseled to get in touch with their own deepest feelings, which were often hidden and conflicted. Then they were to open up to others, preferably in groups; group encounter was the centerpiece of the new method. One of the earliest and most famous engagements between the human potential movement and a Catholic religious order took place in 1965 when the Los Angeles–based Sisters of the Immaculate Heart of Mary (IHM) became involved in a pilot project on the broad-based use of group encounter. William Coulson, himself a devout Catholic and a close associate of Carl Rogers, was for a time project coordinator of the IHM's "Education Innovation Project." Coulson assured the sisters, "When people do what they deeply want to do, it isn't immoral. . . . We have human potential and it's glorious, because we are children of a Loving Creator who has something marvelous in mind for every one of us."[12] The results of the experiment in group encounter were unexpected. Within two years the sisters were deeply divided and involved in a series of well-publicized pitched battles with Cardinal James

MacIntyre of Los Angeles. The IHM experiment sparks controversy to this day.[13]

Here it is important to draw a distinction between the *theory* of humanistic psychology and the *method* of group encounter. It quickly became clear that encounter technique worked as a potent acid burning quickly through layers of protective personal inhibition. It was difficult enough getting in touch with dark emotions, but then to share them in groups without clear limits and close supervision was a formula for unpredictable trouble. Rogers and Coulson declined to repeat the IHM experiment.[14]

The point here is broader than one high-profile example. Rogers and Coulson directed programs for many religious orders of women and men. Rogers alone, for example, was in charge of programs for a number of different groups, including the Sisters of Mercy, the Jesuits, and the Franciscans.[15] This is indicative of the broad and deep impact of humanistic psychology on religious orders, houses of formation, and seminaries. Catholics were searching for newer methods of spiritual formation, and this is what humanistic psychology had to offer.

The theory, on the other hand, worked as a slower solvent, and here its effect in Catholic circles was widespread, sometimes beneficial, but often harmful. Two fateful side effects quickly became evident. First, when the self-actualization model is used, it often empties sinful actions of their objective content. Self-actualizers are set on an expanding continuum of personal growth, and "sins" are regarded as setbacks on the road to ever greater progress. There is only one large sin in this model: the failure to grow. The approach casts a roseate light on wrong human conduct and quickly becomes a caricature of itself. Can one plausibly characterize the problem of Adolf Hitler or Joseph Stalin as a failure to grow? There were no outside measures for self-actualization. In truth, it was a theory of human behavior too positive and optimistic to encompass intractably bad human conduct. It had little time for mortal sin, and no time at all for original sin.

Second, by definition, self-actualization places a low estimate on the value of rules. Rule-bound behavior is other-directed, external compliance to an outside agent. By contrast, the fully actualized person acts from internal motivation. Such persons are a rule unto themselves. For them rules are not necessary and are counter-productive. The only rule is to get in touch with one's feelings and share them with others. Sometimes following such advice involved strange reversals. As attendance at 7:00 a.m. mass became optional, revelations about personal sexuality seemed close to mandatory.

Humanistic psychology would have a large impact on seminary formation after Vatican II. In effect, it helped to fill the vacuum left by the collapse of the Tridentine seminary and the traditional approaches to spirituality and formation that disappeared with it.

THE SEMINARY

The Tridentine Seminary

The final piece of our mosaic concerns the seminary. During this time of transition, the seminary was the institution closest to the fault line, the first place where the tremor that was shortly to strike the priesthood was felt.

The seminary trained and socialized young men for the Catholic priesthood. Introduced by the Council of Trent, a single, unitary system of clergy formation had steadily evolved over the intervening centuries. In many ways, it was emblematic of the post-Reformation Catholic Church and the priesthood.

Seminaries were usually constructed in secluded locations, the better to underscore that they represented a world apart, indeed, a world unto themselves. They were governed by a "rule of life" that minutely regulated the activities of seminarians from their rising to the "grand silence" that closed each day. Seminarians were rarely permitted to leave the grounds, and only with explicit permission. From a sociological point of view, seminaries have regularly been compared to minimum security prisons, but with this difference. Seminarians were taught to regard the rule of life as the will of God. Each tolling of the bell (called the *Vox Dei*, the voice of God) was regarded as a celestial reminder of a duty now at hand.

The resulting atmosphere produced both piety and cynicism. Pious seminarians did regard obedience to the rule as following the will of God. Those who mustered less faith at least knew that the rule was a high-voltage electric fence that created and protected the social reality of the seminary world. Crossing certain well-marked lines rendered a seminarian liable to immediate expulsion. To visit another student's room with the door closed or to leave the grounds without permission constituted lethal breaches of conduct. Since it was the proximate will of God, the rule of life did not have to make sense. It simply had to be obeyed. Indeed, there was greater merit in following it when its practical reason escaped an obedient seminarian.

The seminary deliberately cultivated the quality of an igloo, a place frozen in time. If the church was a timeless, unchanging institution in a changing world, its best and most vivid exemplar was the seminary and its devotion to a rule of life that remained unchanged from one generation to the next. The outside world had little impact on and no point of entry to this self-enclosed world. In the official chronicles of St. Mary's Seminary, Baltimore, which stretch back to 1791, there is not a single reference to the Civil War.[16] The strength of the old seminary was its proud intransigence.

It was also a school of taboos that were silently communicated by example and without explanation. For that reason, no explanation or motivational talk was ever given on celibacy. Such talks would have assumed the church's position needed justification and bolstering, or even worse, that it could change. By contrast, silence on such matters taught students to regard a practice such as celibacy as solid, changeless social reality, a given in the life of a priest, not a human rule but a discipline descended from on high. The rule of life indicated the behaviors that might result in expulsion, and that was all that was said. There were only a few intermediate penalties. Since there was a glut of seminarians, it took no great courage to dismiss a student, and in doubtful cases, the issue was resolved in favor of the church, not the individual. It was seldom clear to other students why someone had been asked to leave. It was rather as if a great arbitrary hand had descended on the seminarian next door and he was gone. Seminarians were dismissed while others were at meals, ensuring their departure had no social impact. Yet while few formal methods of evaluation in a modern sense were employed, seminarians were evaluated on a yearly basis, and the seasoned judgment of the faculty was often shrewd, intuitive, and correct.

The discussion of evaluations and expulsions gives a misleading impression of the pre–Vatican II seminary. In the United States in the 1960s, the seminary drew from the final flowering of Catholic immigrant culture, attracting the brightest and the best. Scholastic philosophy and theology, abstract subjects by any measure, were taught in Latin. The brightest priests were as intelligent and as well educated in a classical vein, as well versed in Latin and Greek literature, as the best of their generation. This was not the average priest, however. At best, 10 to 15 percent fully understood what they were learning. The rest memorized Latin catch-phrases. For them, theology was an expanded version of the *Baltimore Catechism.* The average priest was simply a practical journeyman who followed the rules. The result of this system of education was also a two-tiered clergy of leaders and followers.

The Collapse

In the wake of the council, the great strength of the seminary became at once its Achilles' heel. The rigidity of formation, the sacrosanct quality of the unchanging rule, excluded even the possibility of moderate reform or a flexible response to a new situation. The Tridentine seminary's only response to the tremors of the council was to totter briefly on its foundation and collapse. And the collapse was total.

THE COLLAPSE OF THE SEMINARY

In one venerable seminary in the throes of reform in 1966, a group of seminarians approached the rector about the introduction of a Coca-Cola machine in the student lounge. In refusing this request, the old rector patiently explained to the students the way a father would instruct his children what their request entailed. First they would want a Coke machine. Then they would want candy bars. And how far off could the request be to leave the grounds for pizza?

Then they would have to have cars, wouldn't they? They would inevitably meet young women in the pizza parlor. Some, young and innocent, might invite them back. Then who knows what might happen?

In his mind, the seamless social reality so carefully constructed over generations could be undone by one untoward innovation, the tenuous path from chaos to cosmos destroyed in a careless moment. (In point of fact, the rector was prescient. What he predicted is exactly what happened, and almost in the order he predicted.)

In that same institution a few months later, on a balmy evening in early May, a seminarian heaved a large brick squarely through the window of the room in which the faculty had gathered to evaluate the seminarians. This was an unheard-of gesture of rebellion, yet . . . the old rector was not completely surprised. He knew the request for a Coke machine cloaked something more sinister. He felt in this instant that his world was on the verge of collapse. His worst nightmare was confirmed the next evening when he saw a group of seminarians nonchalantly walking off the seminary grounds. Were they going for pizza? Then the larger truth struck him. The electricity was off on the invisible barriers that prevented the seminarians from leaving the grounds. It was like the scene from Jurassic Park *when the animals discovered the gates were no longer electrified. They simply went out. That same year, the old rector resigned. His world had disappeared. He himself was now a dinosaur, shortly to be swallowed up in the new social reality all around him.*

The collapse of the seminary system in the United States was a national phenomenon. Every seminary, almost without exception, had bad days in the wake of the council, and they were very much the same. Many seminarians and young priests who left the premises were innocent. They had entered the seminary without great forethought and would now be ordained or soon leave the priesthood to get married without sustained reflection in either case. But there were also predatory individuals who left the premises. From their number would come the pedophiles whose stories have filled the newspapers in the past two years. It was not just that the electricity went off in the public fences that surrounded the priesthood.

The electricity went off in people's heads. Priests who would not have dared to omit vespers now stopped saying the breviary entirely. And nothing happened. They were not struck down by a thunderbolt. The rest of the old taboos began to fall, one after another, for priest and people alike.

I think it is hard to overestimate in this context the general impact of the elimination of the Friday fast. This law had obliged Catholics under the pain of mortal sin, a hanging offense by any measure. Catholic imagination had long been nourished by the vision of wayward Catholics banished to hell or, at least, to purgatory for a long stretch of hard time because they had wantonly eaten meat on Friday. Many Catholics who had not darkened the doors of a church in years kept the Friday fast. Catholics did not know the discipline could change. And then, with the stroke of a pen, the Friday fast became optional. What of the Catholics who were languishing in the netherworld on this score? Were they as suddenly released? Above all, if this rule could be change, then was anything immune from reversal? Truly, the old rules did not seem to apply. A new age had dawned.

The church had heretofore regarded itself as a timeless, embattled citadel in a hostile, changing world and, in the United States, an immigrant church in a largely Protestant, unfriendly society. Now this relationship shifted 180 degrees. The deliberately chosen opening words of the Pastoral Constitution on the Church in the Modern World (1965) conveyed the new message: *Gaudium et Spes*, joy and hope. The church shares the joys and hopes of the modern world and turns toward it now in a friendly, welcoming way. The new seminary followed suit.

The Seminary after the Council

The decade and a half after the close of the council in 1965 were not easy years for Catholic seminaries. The one bright, steady light was intellectual formation. In the wake of conciliar documents *Dei Verbum* (Dogmatic Constitution on Divine Revelation, 1965), *Lumen Gentium* (Dogmatic Constitution on the Church, 1964), and *Optatam Totius* (Decree on Priestly Formation, 1965) the academic quality of seminary formation improved dramatically.

By contrast, the formational and evaluative components virtually disappeared. No surprise then that seminary formation, abbreviated to its academic component, was often reduced in the early 1970s to a three-year in-house program, followed by a pastoral internship. Here the seminarian, usually a deacon, was placed in a parish often as much at sea as the seminary he'd come from. Older seminary personnel, much like the old rector we've just met, had lost their nerve for evaluation. They resembled the former caretakers of *Jurassic Park*, now lost souls themselves. New faculty members were themselves children of the age, not unlike the seminarians. Seismic tremors were felt all around. The number of seminarians plummeted between 1967–68 and 1980–81. There were 8,159 theologians in 1967 and 4,187 in 1980, a drop of almost 50 percent.[17] At the same time, the number of priests leaving active ministry rose dramatically, spiking in 1968 (525), 1970 (675), and 1973 (575).[18] There was a symmetry to these numbers, and they delivered a simple message. The priesthood was a vocation one could, perhaps should abandon. The smart money was moving out, not in.

In lieu of screening and firm evaluation, the growth method with its soft edges was widely introduced. In particular, sexual experimentation by seminarians was dealt with very gently. A degree of sexual acting out was tolerated that ten years before or ten years later was unthinkable. Sometimes faculty themselves were involved. Hence in the ten years following the council, those who wanted to be ordained, got ordained. Institutional vetoes were absent or ineffective, couched in terms of self-actualization theory that could neutralize negative factors by placing them on the long continuum of human growth. Here a second set of potential sexual abusers, different from the first, entered the priesthood, the second source from which the current scandals drew.

It is fair to say that an important reason many men left the priesthood after the council was celibacy. They left to get married. Concomitantly the number of homosexual priests and seminarians probably increased.[19] Seminaries suddenly began to develop gay subcultures that encompassed faculty and students. New men entering the seminary were often disillusioned by what they found, a pale but clear reflection of the sexual behavior that held sway in the wider culture.

The period can be dated with some precision. The most diffi-cult years were 1967 to 1980. For more than a decade, for the same and for different reasons, the seminary and the priesthood seemed to lose their bearings. If there was one large factor that abetted this lateral drift, it was the outstanding issue of celibacy. The papacy of Paul VI had seemingly shot its last effective bolt in 1968 with *Humanae Vitae;* although his papacy lasted for another decade, it could no longer answer big questions with a firm and authoritative voice.[20] Nowhere was this more evident than in re-gard to the discipline of celibacy and its continuance, despite the fact that Paul VI had issued an encyclical on the subject in 1967, *Sacerdotalis Coelibatus.*

If the discipline was going to change and the change was immi-nent, then why bother with the current seminary in its confused state? The seminary socializes men into the Catholic priesthood; if the priesthood was shortly going to be a married one, seminary formation would need to be scrapped whole and entire, and then revamped from top to bottom.

The seminary system languished until the election of John Paul II in 1978 and his firm decision to put the considerable weight of his papacy behind the discipline of celibacy. It was only then that the seminary system was taken seriously. It is no surprise that within three years of his election, John Paul II ordered a papal visitation of United States seminaries (1981). If celibacy was to remain, a crucial decision had been made about the shape of seminary formation for the future.

TROUBLED YEARS

Exactly ten years after the incident with the Coke machine, a dis-turbing incident occurred over spring recess at a large seminary in the Midwest. A janitor, cleaning what he thought were empty student rooms, discovered two seminarians in bed together. He re-ported the matter with disgust to an older priest he knew well. The man received the information philosophically. He had recently been reading about such cases. He presumed that these young men were growing, coming to terms with their sexuality, and had fallen into "inappropriate" behavior. He had learned to use the word "inappropriate" where he used to say "bad," "wrong," or "immoral." He still thought of it as bad, wrong, and immoral, but perhaps that was just him. He certainly hoped they were speaking with their advisors. He brought the matter to a younger faculty member who would better understand such problems. He likewise took the news philosophically. Such behavior was very troubling. The students would have to deal with the incident. The young men were engaged in a process of discernment and might use the incident as a kairos *moment toward greater personal integration on the road to the priesthood. In neither case was there any thought of dismissal.*

Privately the younger priest had other thoughts. He knew the students quite well. They were gay. The young priest was gay. He had met them with still other students in a well-known bar that catered to a gay clientele. He wondered if he was compromised. He didn't think so, but then again, he could not be sure. All the more reason to deal with the matter gently and not stir this pot too vigorously. Then he thought of other students, indeed, of other priests he knew and what he could only describe as their lack of discretion. Their behavior was so, and here he groped for the right word . . . so inappropriate.

DRAWING THE THREADS TOGETHER: MAKING SENSE OF THE SCANDALS

This is the right point in the narrative to turn to the question with which we began. How to make sense of the sexual abuse scandals? We can approach the question from two angles. It is possible to focus on the cases of abuse and generalize about the church from which they sprang. The opposite tack keeps us closer to the question. Beginning with the priesthood as a whole, what were the conditions in the church and society that allowed cases of sexual abuse to arise in such numbers at this time? What was the state of the priesthood twenty-five years ago from which the lion's share of the scandals originated?

On January 12, 2003, the *New York Times* assembled a study from church documents, court records, news reports, and interviews.[21] Although not definitive, this study represented the most exhaustive data to date on sexual abuse by priests. The study extended from 1950 through December 31, 2002. It counted 1,205 documented cases of sexual abuse involving 1.8 percent of priests ordained in that time frame. In capsule form: "Most of the abuse occurred in the 1970s and 1980s, the survey found. The number of priests accused of abuse declines sharply by the 1990s."[22] The concentration of cases by decades reveals 256 cases of abuse in the 1960s, 537 in the 1970s, 510 in the 1980s, 211 in the 1990s.[23]

For our purposes, the most significant part of the study is the parallel drawn between the cases of abuse and the ordination class of the abusers. The largest numbers of abusers were ordained in the years before and just after the council. The numbers begin to rise in the late 1950s. The largest spike occurs in the 1970s. "More known offenders were ordained in the 1970s than in any other decade."[24] What is the profile of the victims? Eighty percent were male, 57 percent were teenagers, 6 percent were younger than the age of twelve.[25]

EMPIRICAL DATA

When this book was in the last stages before publication, two long-awaited studies on priestly sexual abuse appeared. On February 27, 2004, the National Review Board for the Protection of Children and Young People of the American Bishops published "A Report on the Crisis in the Catholic Church in the United States." The Review Board had commissioned a study by the John Jay College of Criminal Justice, "The Nature and Scope of the Problem of Sexual Abuse of Minors by Catholic Priests and Deacons in the United States," which was released the same day. The John Jay College study presented the empirical data. The Review Board supplied an interpretative analysis. For our purposes, three statistics stand out.

First, the study sets the percentage of priests accused of sexual abuse at 4 percent over fifty-two years. This is more than double the figure cited in the New York Times study of January 12, 2003. Since these crimes are often under-reported, the final number could rise.

Second, the latest study confirms what now should be seen as a given. The crisis of priestly sexual abuse reached epidemic proportions in the 1970s. The word "epidemic" is used advisedly; in the ordination class of 1970, one priest in ten faced an allegation of sexual abuse. Then the number of incidents declined sharply in the next two decades, more sharply than the rate of increase in the 1960s and 1970s.

Third, 81 percent of the victims were male. Just as it is perilous to merge priestly sexual abuse with the larger topic of homosexuality in the clergy, it is equally impossible to separate the two.

The Priesthood Demystified

In redefining the Eucharist, Vatican II's liturgical reforms also redrew the role of the priest. In one sense, he is no less central today. But he is central in a different way, surrounded now by other liturgical ministers and an active congregation. A conscious *demystification* of the priesthood, however, was part and parcel of this shift. The priest is less a sacred person now, an *alter Christus,* "another Christ," celebrating the mass that others silently attend. Now he has become a *primus inter pares,* "the first among equals" with other ministers.

Priestly conduct was regulated and held together by taboos that stretched from the Eucharist to the outer reaches of priestly life down to the simple salutation, "Father." These taboos were effective barriers against certain conduct. When such barriers fall, they are not automatically replaced by moral or ethical constraints. To the contrary, moral constraints operate in another frame of reference. When taboos fall, they are frequently replaced by nothing at all.

Furthermore, it was not as if one taboo fell and others held. They all fell together. Once the priesthood was demystified at the altar, the movement spread to other domains of priestly life, lowering barriers and inhibitions on heretofore forbidden activities. In this regard, priestly conduct was not first regulated by moral restraint. It may have played a role, but it was not the chief motivator. The motivation lay in the realm of taboo, the fear of being struck by a thunderbolt or its equivalent, the stab of immobilizing fear that kept scrupulous priests endlessly reciting the Words of Institution and just as endlessly failing to complete them. But once the magic circle is broken, there are few limits and surely not, at first, moral ones.

Moral Boundaries and the Growth Imperative

Priests were also the first to know that moral theology now suggested more nuanced rules. It is not hard to imagine that priests may often have been the first to act on them. If premoral barriers had fallen, the moral limits themselves were now more flexible and forgiving. The older classification of objectively sinful acts now gave way to broader theories that encompassed a range of human motivation. Did this action imperil a person's fundamental option for God, Christ, and the church? Such a question is very hard to answer, and that may be the point. In the land of broad intentions, there are few effective restraints on what a person specifically wants to do. In regard to the cultural revolution, it is not as if priests reluctantly followed in the rearguard. No, they sometimes led the way.

Here as well, theories of personal self-actualization fell on fertile ground. If personal self-actualization means getting in touch with one's feelings, surely that includes sexual feelings. If acting on such feelings is part of one's personal growth trajectory, then such conduct is not forbidden. Indeed, it may be recommended, the right thing to do. In this regard, enlightened theological opinion in Europe and the United States after Vatican II quickly and almost unanimously concluded that mandatory celibacy for diocesan clergy no longer made sense. It belonged to the model of the priesthood that Vatican II had consigned to the past, a vestige of a bygone era. A change in the discipline seemed imminent. If celibacy was shortly to fall, can there be much harm in anticipating the event, especially when it seems an important part of one's personal growth plan?

As premoral barriers to sexual experimentation fell and moral barriers were lowered, other voices were actively encouraging such behavior. When the full force of change in sexual mores struck the discipline of celibacy, now without theological justification, the effects were devastating. The pattern of sexual abuse by priests in the 1970s needs to be placed in a much wider context of sexual experimentation by priests across the board in those same years. The great majority of cases did not sink to the level of abuse. But the experimentation did provide a fertile seedbed for the latter. There were simply very few good reasons to prevent priests so inclined from experimenting with sex. Once again, if Catholics blended into the general pattern of American culture, priests were no exception. The only effective barriers were the memories of the past and a widespread gut feeling on the part of many priests that something was wrong with this new picture.

It now seems relatively clear why the incidents of sexual abuse emerging from this milieu clustered around two cadres of priests. The first are those ordained in the 1950s and 1960s before the council. They may have been sexual abusers in any case, but the new climate after Vatican II was now more favorable to giving those instincts free play. The largest group of abusers were ordained in the 1970s, and this make sense too. These were children of the age who passed through a seminary system that was not capable of stopping them. Many acted out in the seminary and simply continued the behavior after ordination. Some never made an attempt to lead a celibate life or reinterpreted celibacy for their own purposes. The difference between the two groups is clear enough. The first may have had inhibitions and lost them; the second probably had few inhibitions to begin with.

The Church and Reform

The broadest context of these scandals is the church and the reforms of Vatican II that occurred a scant ten years before the worst outbreak of sexual abuse by priests. It had been the proud boast of the church that in an ever changing world, it remained always the same, *semper idem*, the motto of conservative Cardinal Alfredo Ottaviani, staunch opponent of progressive reform at Vatican II.

It should come as no surprise that when a church so self-styled does undertake reforms, it enters virgin territory. In one sense, it was fortunate in its first venture. In most organizations, when a command is given from the top, it is muffled and thwarted by layers of staff and bureaucracy. But when the pope in council with the entire Catholic episcopate effected the reforms of Vatican II, the church at this special moment in its history saluted and followed orders. It is hard to imagine it happening again. One need only reflect on the decades, indeed the centuries, it required for the Council of Trent to carry through its decisions.

But there was large collateral damage. If the church spun swiftly on its axis at Vatican II, the brunt of the pivot was borne in large measure by the priesthood. As the bishops were declared to represent the fullness of the priesthood and the laity were empowered, the priesthood lay squarely in the path of these progressive turns. The priesthood went into the Second Vatican Council universally acclaimed as the lead horse of the church's mission. Consequently, it was also the first to feel the tremors in the shift toward a newer vision of church.

The change in the fortunes of the priesthood in three generations is almost unimaginable. The steady workhorse vocation of the preconciliar era had come to play the role of hero and villain in the postconciliar world. Priests remained the foot soldiers of the reforms of Vatican II, but as major perpetrators of the sexual abuse of children, they now are major villains too.

It will take much more time and distance, prayer and reflection to understand fully why the sexual abuse of children by priests rose so dramatically at this time in the church's history. Perhaps sexual abuse existed at this rate all along but was hidden in the cloak of silence surrounding priests. But I believe it happened at this time in such numbers for specific reasons, and I have assembled those reasons as best I understand them. I should also be honest about the limits of this analysis. Explaining how permissive attitudes on heterosexual and homosexual activity grew up among priests does not answer the final question about why the sexual abuse of children happened. That topics rests with abnormal psychology, and I cannot presume to offer an answer here. Pending more complete data, the explanation of the scandals remains a tentative, indeed a speculative venture. But the work must begin at some point, however inadequate the first attempts. Otherwise, without some understanding, the sexual abuse scandals remain in the history of the priesthood as a large, undigested clot. Moreover, those who do not understand the past are more likely to repeat it, and certainly much less likely to move beyond its mistakes with honesty and integrity.

Reason for Hope

Just as the collapse of the seminary was a national phenomenon, so too was its rebuilding. After the initial euphoria of release from the Tridentine seminary, it soon became apparent to faculty and staff that they were, in effect, sitting in the rubble of a fallen institution. It did not constitute a new system. The patient, tedious, and arduous work of rebuilding had to begin. Better initial screening and better formation were essential although neither was easy, given the dwindling pool of seminarians. Probably everyone's standards were lower than they cared to admit. But at least there were *some* standards.

Accordingly, the air of unreality that hung over the seminary in the 1970s began to lift. There had to be rules. Topics like sexuality and celibacy had to be consciously and specifically addressed. Unfit seminarians had to be screened out or dismissed. The rebuilding phase of the seminary is still in its first stages, and it should not make too many claims. But it can claim positive achievements.

External pressure also played a role. The Vatican visitation of U.S. seminaries that began in 1981 continued throughout the decade, concluding in 1990. Under the direction of Bishop John Marshall, assisted by then Father (now Bishop) Donald Wuerl, the visitation combined sensitivity and firmness. The visitation teams were comprised of American bishops and seminary personnel. An important by-product of this approach was a common pool of assumptions and a growing consensus about the direction seminaries should take. The decade closed with an international Synod on Priestly Formation in 1990. The postsynodal exhortation, *Pastores*

Dabo Vobis (1992), is widely regarded as the most significant statement on priestly formation that the Holy See has issued in recent history. It has received a positive welcome by an unusually wide spectrum of audiences. With rare unanimity, bishops and seminary personnel regard it as a charter document on priestly formation that can dependably guide the church into the third millennium. The fourth edition of the U.S. *Program of Priestly Formation* was issued the same year.[26] Noticeably slimmer than earlier editions, this document sought to balance earlier emphases. Each section also ended with a clear set of norms. The document suggested another round of visitations in order to certify that individual American seminaries were in compliance with the new norms.

It should be clear that the seminary has been under steady, consistent reconstruction for more than two decades, and these efforts have not been without fruit.

A PERSONAL NOTE

I served as rector of St. Patrick's Seminary, the archdiocesan seminary for San Francisco, from 1978 to 1988. This was like being on board, sometimes in charge of, a ship passing through a hurricane. After a brief stint at the USCCB, I served as rector of the Theological College of the Catholic University of America from 1992 to 2002. The students at Theological College in my final year, 2002, were by far the best and healthiest group of seminarians I had encountered in a long career. I took this as a comment on them, but equally on the priests who inspired such vocations in the first place — for me proof positive that the priesthood, after some rough years, was settling down. Then in January of that year, the revelations of sexual abuse of children by priests began to tumble out of Boston and other dioceses. It was hard for me to gauge the seminarians' reaction. Frankly, I think I took it worse than they did. They seemed to absorb these events like the news of a distant family member, clearly family, but not close, who had been thrown in jail. It was for me, in Dickens's phrase, the best of times and the worst of times, cheek-by-jowl together.

FINAL THOUGHTS

The priesthood is sounder and in better shape that one might conclude from the stories of priestly misconduct that have steadily
appeared in the media in recent years. The cases of sexual abuse
occurred in large measure a generation ago. Like the Perfect Storm,
a constellation of factors in the immediate wake of a great council
rendered the Catholic priesthood especially vulnerable at that moment. I think those conditions have passed. It is no accident that
the incidences of abuse fell sharply in the 1990s. The priesthood is
settling down, albeit as a smaller cadre of men with larger infusions
of ethnic vocations. Clearly priests are now demoralized by having
to digest again and take responsibility for some of the worst moments in their collective history, accepting as well the shadow of
suspicion that those events cast across them still. But underneath
this, there is considerable strength. In concluding this discussion
of the scandals, three truths loom large.

First, in the present climate, the discipline of celibacy will not
change. Celibacy is a discipline; it could change. Theologically,
the priesthood is equally compatible with marriage. But the current scandals have politicized the issue, linking celibacy to the
priesthood at every point. I also doubt that the U.S. church in
the trough of the wave could muster the resolve to undertake the
bold move to a married clergy. Doubtful, too, that the Holy See
would permit such a change in the midst of turmoil. From many
points of view, this does not seem a propitious time for large-scale
experimentation.

Second, while the sexual abuse scandals make sense only in the
context of Vatican II and the postconciliar era, once placed there,
these scandals turn around and make a comment on the reforms
of Vatican II. Was the council somehow to blame? Was it scapegoat,
bystander, or culprit in these events? One way or another, what
impact will the sexual abuse scandals have on the reforms of Vatican II? In what spirit will these reforms be carried into their second
and third generation?

In regard to the continuance of Vatican II, a negative response to
a major ecumenical council is in a sense unthinkable for Catholics

who know their faith and take it seriously. If it happened at all, such a response would not be explicit or deliberate. Rather like soldiers leaving a battlefield, people might drift off one by one or in small groups, abandoning the effort. The reforms of Vatican II would languish. A positive response, on the other hand, would be conscious and deliberate, requiring a large measure of courage. But a positive response in the present situation also carries the prospect of a renewed sense of purpose. The priesthood needs something positive to pull it into the future. Embracing the challenge of the council anew offers this pull. The reforms of Vatican II will require the best efforts of priests and people over five or six generations to bring them to fruition. In God's providence, the priesthood has been put to a severe test one generation into this voyage.

Lastly, I fear that the talk of structural change may obscure the deeper fact that a dilemma of this proportion requires a spiritual solution. Priests and bishops whose integrity has been so deeply questioned can overcome such difficulties only by reaching into their own deepest resources. The challenge is radical; the response must be radical as well. "If any want to become my follower, let them deny themselves and take up their cross daily and follow me. For those who want to save their life will lose it, and those who lose their life for my sake will save it" (Luke 9:23–24). I think Jesus's words were meant to be taken literally. Only in hard times is that clear. But when that is clear, the rest will follow.

Chapter Two

THIS GENERATION OF SEMINARIANS, THIS GENERATION OF SEMINARIES

I N UPDATING THE FORMATION of Catholic priests worldwide, the Second Vatican Council suggested a formula that has been successfully followed for four decades.[1] The Council (later, the Congregation for Catholic Education) establishes general guidelines. Each episcopal conference makes those guidelines more specific, adapting them to the pastoral needs of the church, region by region throughout the world. Subject to the approval of the Holy See, such national guidelines are revised at regular intervals. In this way, the church has attempted to balance unity and diversity in the training of future clergy.

In adapting priestly formation to ongoing pastoral needs, the council's formula also tacitly recognized that there may be factors beyond anyone's control that affect priestly formation in every way. Two such stand out at present. First, the kind of men drawn to the priesthood. What kind of person enters a seminary these days? Second, on the other end, what are the parishes like into which newly ordained priests are sent? How large is the average parish? Then, depending on region, what is its ethnic composition? Where will priests live, and how will they be supported in their vocation?

While statistical trends indicating the size and ethnic composition of parishes seem relatively clear, the answer to the first question is less certain and involves more imponderables. Still, these two questions need to be acknowledged early and together, because they form the bedrock assumptions about how best to train candidates for the priesthood. And in spite of the difficulties, some portrait of the present seminarian needs to be assembled, however uncertain and imprecise its details may be.

THIS GENERATION OF SEMINARIANS: THE CHILDREN OF COLLAGE CATHOLICISM

What is different about this generation of seminarians? First, they are fewer in number. In 2001/2002, there were 2,621 diocesan seminarians in theology in the last stages of formation for the priesthood. In 1990/1991, there were 2,516. The number of diocesan seminarians remained stable for the decade of the 1990s. In actuality, the picture has remained roughly the same for the last two decades. That fact has been registered but deserves repetition. The precipitous decline occurred between 1967 and 1980. The number of religious seminarians has shown less stability. Nevertheless, the same ten-year totals, though posting some decline, are not far apart: 963 religious candidates in 2001/2002 compared to 1,057 in 1990/1991. Ominously, in 2002/2003 the first year after the major revelations of priestly sexual abuse, seminary enrollment declined by 5 percent.[2]

Frequently the problem of dwindling numbers is misstated. For example, the comparison between the *total* number of seminarians in 1967/1968 and the *total* number in 2001/2002 is misleading, because it does not sufficiently acknowledge that the college and high school seminaries have largely dropped from the picture.[3] In other words, the traditional three-stage feeder system for the priesthood — four years of high school, four years of college, four years of theology; in at age thirteen, ordained at age twenty-five — simply collapsed in the wake of Vatican II. The more telling statistic is the number of men in the last stages of formation these days as compared to the same number at the high-water mark of vocations in the late 1960s. There were 4,875 diocesan seminarians in theology in 1967/1968. There are 2,489 in 2002/2003. The decline of religious vocations in the same period is sharper: 3,283 in 1967/1968 compared to 925 in 2002/2003.[4]

This represents tempered good news with unalloyed bad news. The good news is that the priesthood is still a functioning vocation, a viable calling. Men are entering the seminary and being ordained in smaller yet still significant numbers. The real problem comes into focus when the *decline* in priesthood candidates is set against the *rise* in the number of Catholics they serve. Catholics represent 22 percent of the population, bringing the current number of Catholics in the United States to 62.2 million.[5] Many fewer priests must serve many more Catholics. Further, the church in the United States faces an anomalous situation. Normally vocations to the priesthood and religious life are an index of the vitality of the local church. But while the American church flourishes in many ways, it has not produced a corresponding harvest of vocations in more than a generation. This fact alone will shape the future face of the church in countless ways.

What are seminarians like these days? They sometimes refer to themselves as the children of *collage Catholicism.* Often bright and well educated, their faith almost uniformly lacks content or firm contour. The Catholicism they learned as children consisted largely of sets of images and attitudes. A tinge of resentment often lingers. A generation ago candidates entered the seminary with the residue of the *Baltimore Catechism.* It was possible for them to see, for example, how the documents of Vatican II shifted the received tradition. In the past, seminarians had a contoured brain and a rudimentary capacity for theological discernment. Now the surface is smooth. Such students want to learn the official teaching of the church because they sense (and here they are right) that their native capacity for theological discernment is not well developed. The perceptual grid has few lines. And when they think of theologians, beginning seminarians do not think of Avery Dulles or Karl Rahner; they think of what they have read in the newspaper or *Time* magazine. They think of the "Jesus Seminar" and the occasional theologian who gains fleeting notoriety. Some describe the current generation as conservative. I am not sure what word I would use. Most of them are still in the process of trying to learn the names of the pieces on the chessboard. Frankly, theological education would be greatly enhanced if they could swallow a copy of the *Catechism*

of the Catholic Church whole and entire. That at least would provide a common set of markers with which the study of theology
could begin. Mine may represent a minority voice, but I think the
task in seminary education has sometimes slipped from theology
to catechism. This holds true for self-styled conservative and liberal seminarians alike. Common ignorance far outweighs surface
posturing to the right or the left.

So-called "Collage Catholicism" has a second face. Along with
the hunger for doctrinal content, another yearning appears. The
liturgical reforms of the Second Vatican Council in the second
generation of their reception have produced a hunger for popular
devotions that the liturgical renewal at first disparaged, such as eucharistic adoration, public recitation of the rosary, stations of the
cross, and novenas. Among seminarians, such devotional concerns
are sometimes coupled with an interest in the accouterments of
preconciliar priesthood, e.g., amices, palls, cassocks, and birettas.
Such interests are perplexing, if not downright offputting, to older
priests who were happy to shed such items a generation ago.

A sympathetic assessment of this second face would note that the
clean, spare liturgy of Vatican II has scarcely had time to cultivate its
own type of popular devotion. Yet the Catholic imagination among
the young and the pious of this generation remains relentlessly
analogical, sacramental, and symbolic, seeking tangible expression
in signs and symbols. In this in-between stage, Catholic liturgy
without its customary fringe of popular devotion has sometimes
been dubbed "low-cal Catholicism." Whatever the nomenclature,
the current generation of seminarians often feels as if it were raised
on a sparse diet of sacramental signs, symbols, and devotional practices. They are probably right. But it is another matter whether they
compensate for the spare diet in appropriate ways.

Is it possible to describe the emerging face of a new generation
of Roman Catholic priests, the first of this millennium? I think
not, or at least not yet. The above analysis does not sufficiently
incorporate the changing ethnic face of the Catholic priesthood —
the number of future priests, for example, born outside the United
States. Besides, whatever indices now exist will need to be reevalu-
ated in light of the impact of the sexual abuse scandals. That card

is still face down. To sum up the issues in positive terms, the current generation of seminarians registers a strong desire for doctrinal content in theology as well as a hunger for prayer and devotional practice. Whether these become the hallmark of a new generation of Catholic priest remains to be seen.

What Hans Urs von Balthasar wrote about Mariology may be instructive in regard to the priesthood at this time. He spoke of the "ebb and flow through history of Mariology's tides; a flood of lofty attributes, titles, and veneration is almost necessarily followed by an ebb that restores the level; but the ebb-tide can also seep away, leading to a forgetfulness that is unworthy of theology."[6] Does the same oscillation characterize the priesthood as well? There have been ages in which the priest has been seen as a man set apart, an *alter Christus*. Other ages have seen him first as a member of the Christian community, *primus inter pares,* a first among equals with other Christian ministers. While noting the distinction that *Lumen Gentium* 10 carefully appends, Vatican II a generation ago chose to emphasize the latter. Is the pendulum now swinging in the other direction? Only time will tell.

VOCATIONS

Recent seminarians often portray the story of their vocation as an uphill struggle in which their interest in the priesthood met with mixed reactions from fellow Catholics — sometimes an encouraging word, but just as often a discouraging one. Their stories remind one of the familiar line about ships passing in the night: the church searches for vocations; vocations search for the church; neither party knows how to connect.

But beyond the question of reception, timeless features about vocations stand out.

Invariably, a vocation begins with a small, inner voice asking, "Am I called to be a priest?" Seldom is that voice greeted with enthusiasm. Most people wish it would go away. But it does not. Though the voice is small, it has a stubborn persistence far out of proportion to its faint timbre. This means that eventually one must speak with another person about it. That *first* other person is seldom a parent and almost never a vocation director. The parental voice speaks with too much authority for such a tender sprout. Speaking to a vocation director betokens an inchoate decision. The first person is usually a neutral figure, a better testing ground for a tentative thought. Gradually the prospect is tested with others. The reactions are often mixed and sometimes surprising. Some have sensed it all along; they are sure the aspiration fits the person. Others are puzzled or cautious. Sometimes parents are pleased. But sometimes not. No wonder candidates wait to tell them.

Then the candidate enters a period of debate. Do I act on the voice or not? Here his options may be more limited than he realizes. If he does *not* act on the possibility of a vocation that has grown in him over a period of years, it can blight other vocational choices. The voice may persist, "You could have been a priest. That is what God was calling you do to. You could have been more and better than whatever you are doing right now." If the thought lingers, it invariably casts a disparaging shadow on other choices. The better, more difficult choice is to act on the voice. Even if a man finds out at close range that the priesthood is not for him, he may rest more easily with that outcome. He will also have the satisfaction of knowing that he took a possible call from God seriously. A call from God is always serious business and never to be taken lightly.

It is important to underscore the church's traditional conviction that a vocation is a call from God that the church ratifies. The social climate may encourage or discourage a positive response, but that is not the issue. A vocation is a deep and mysterious interior call that can never be fully explained. It is also a stubborn, persistent seed that can grow in rocky soil, an important thought to keep in mind in the wake of recent scandals. Long term, it is uncertain what effect they will have on vocations, because it is not clear as yet how the church will respond. Short term, they can only constitute a hovering, dark cloud. But good or bad, *external factors,* as significant as they may be, are not in the final analysis the determinant of an *interior voice.* That became clear two generations ago when all the social signals about the priesthood were favorable. After World War II, in the wake of *Going My Way,* and *The Bells of St. Mary's,* when Hollywood's favorite actors, Spencer Tracy and Bing Crosby, played the roles of a priests and Thomas Merton's *Seven Storey Mountain* topped the bestseller list, men entered seminaries and monasteries in large numbers, only to discover a few years later that neither Thomas Merton's compelling story nor the ingenuity of Cecil B. DeMille could supply that interior voice.

But this much is clear now. The way in which the church confronts the current crisis will determine a new social climate that will either encourage or discourage vocations in new ways. The era of 1990 to 2001 showed a relative stabilization of vocations to the priesthood. That situation has now changed, and the first news about seminary enrollment after the scandals is not encouraging. But this is just the beginning.

THIS GENERATION OF SEMINARY

The kind of men attracted to the priesthood and the kind of parishes they serve will determine the face of seminary education in the decades ahead.

Certainly because of the differences in age (the beginning age is about thirty), education, and ethnic background of seminarians, a one-size-fits-all seminary program will not work.[7] The development of the "pretheologate" — a program for candidates with no academic training or spiritual formation, entering the seminary for the first time — is a good example of the system's adaptation to the diverse needs of entering candidates. It also strikes a more general note. Seminary formation in this generation must be more individually tailored. If this is true in academics, it is more true in regard to personal and spiritual formation.

Furthermore, two generations ago, a man ordained at age twenty-five in a large diocese looked forward to a twenty-year apprenticeship as a curate before becoming a pastor. That situation has radically changed. In many dioceses, a newly ordained priest can expect a stint of three to five years before he becomes a pastor. This has direct implications for the seminary. The seminary must endeavor to train men not just as priests but as *pastors* almost from the start.

These two factors will radically affect not only how seminary programs are structured but also the qualities one wishes to encourage (or discourage) in seminarians. The question of structure comes to a head in a special way in regard to the seminary community, a highly potent factor in seminary formation. How closely or loosely knit should the seminary community be structured? For entering students brought up in a culture of individual choice and often forced to nourish the thought of the priesthood and the spiritual life on their own, the seminary community appears like an oasis to a thirsty man. It is a great relief and a deep support to enter, usually for the first time, a community of like-minded men who share the same ideals and aspirations. Such a community naturally becomes the seedbed in which genuine formation can occur. It also gives tangible expression to a fundamental truth: the priesthood is a corporate charism before it belongs to any individual, a communal charism that incorporates each person into a worldwide order of priests. These are heady truths in an individualistic age.

Together, seminarians form a community of prayer, the *sine qua non* for the development of individual prayer life. Beginning with prayer, the seminarians form a community of formation in which all the topics that hold together priestly life — prayer, celibacy, sexuality, obedience, authority, co-responsibility — need to be consciously and deliberately addressed and publicly articulated to the community as a whole. Then the same subjects need to be appropriated individually, with the help of an advisor and a spiritual director.

In short, what in an earlier age was communicated by example and silent taboo must now be brought to the level of articulate speech. Everyone together must first hear the same thing at the same time on important topics, e.g., celibacy. Then individual appropriation must follow. The ultimate intent is clear. The seminary must endeavor to bring the seminarian to deliberately, consciously, and freely choose the elements that constitute a priestly way of life. The seminary can harbor no illusions, however. Individual choice in a sea of social permissiveness is a fragile craft. Hence, in the seminary, the individual choices of seminarians in regard to celibate living must be reinforced by like-minded choices and like-minded behavior by others in the same community. The existence of sub-cultures is inevitable, but they cannot represent alternate lifestyles without undermining the seminary as a whole. Likewise, in a diocese later on, an individual priest must feel that his own behavior is reflected and supported by similar attitudes and behaviors in fellow priests. It should be clear from recent events that every seminarian and priest is responsible for himself and co-responsible for his confrères. The behavior of one reflects on the reputation of all. It also will become increasingly evident that if one does not choose to live a celibate life with integrity, it is better, cleaner, and more honest to leave the seminary. It is also a kindness to others who seek to live such a commitment with integrity. Deliberate personal choice surrounded by communities that support such choices is the only way a priestly way of life is communicated, and the only way it is sustained.

A community of formation is also the locus for theological education and the place where pastoral skills are acquired and honed. On an informal level, the give-and-take between seminarians in formation is of inestimable importance on every level. It is no surprise that seminary years are the source of long and sustained friendships among priests that form the basis of support over a lifetime. For the same reason, the general health of the seminary community is of paramount concern. It may sound like an abstract quantum but, in reality, it is exactly the opposite, most obvious in its absence. An unhealthy community gives off an odor, noticeable even to a casual passerby.

Yet upon ordination, diocesan priests increasingly live alone or briefly with one other priest. The issue of community living clearly separates the formation of diocesan priests from that of religious. Dominicans, Franciscans, Benedictines, and Jesuits either live in a community or are in close contact with their communities. There is more continuity between the circumstances of their formation as seminarians and their living conditions as priests. For diocesan priests, the opposite is true. But doesn't this represent a serious dilemma? *If a healthy, vibrant community is a key ingredient in the formation of diocesan priests, might that same factor unwittingly render young priests dysfunctional for the kind of living situations they usually enter after ordination?*

A SERIOUS DILEMMA

A seminary rector visits the bishop of a local diocese, a thoughtful man with long experience. He asks the bishop about his experience with the newly ordained. The bishop ponders his answer carefully, mentally going through the list of those ordained in the last five years. "Ouch," he almost says aloud when his mind lights on one or two young priests. He turns to the rector, carefully framing his answer.

He begins positively, "Father, let me say first of all that we are delighted by your efforts. We have generally been quite pleased with our newly ordained priests. But if I were to note one quality we have noticed that gives us some pause, it is that they seem to be, well... fragile. Will they hold up long term?

"I also know that seminarians are surrounded by advisors and a spiritual director and occasionally a psychotherapist for five or six years — and don't misunderstand, I'm all for it, if that is called for. On any Friday, they also have forty or fifty friends around. Then with ordination, all that ends. The support systems are removed."

He squints, collects his thoughts, and, after a moment, continues. "I hope you don't take offense at the image. A bishop friend sometimes compares newly ordained priests to patients emerging from a long-term intensive care unit. Just as the patient is plugged into five or six IV's, so the seminarian is attached to an elaborate support system. Then all at once the tubes are removed. I worry about what happens afterward."

The bishop is right to be worried. The gap between seminary life and normal rectory living presents a dilemma of major proportions and it is not clear what should be done about it. The seminary and diocese should probably begin by splitting responsibility down the middle. The seminary should strive to develop a community of formation, but not one so closely knit as to render newly ordained priests less functional for the kind of ministry they are entering. For its part, the diocese must at once begin serious programs for the newly ordained. The dilemma underscores a single conclusion: initial formation and ongoing clergy formation must be joined at every point. This is not first of all a matter of formal theological education, as significant as that may be, but rather of personal and spiritual formation. The diocese must accept major responsibility because that is where the priest will minister for the rest of his life.

The heart of the matter may simply be the way diocesan priests are increasingly forced to live — alone, largely unsupported, and prone to the temptations of a lonely life, ranging from food and alcohol to sex and pornography. Perhaps knowledge of the dilemma will act as a spur for dioceses to organize viable communal living arrangement for priests in which their spiritual and personal needs are better cared for.

Since men are now trained not just as priests but as pastors, that must also determine the qualities that should be encouraged (and discouraged) in their formation. Clearly for a ministry as open-ended and multifaceted as the average parish, seminarians should be encouraged to be independent self-starters. A range of other talents are called for. An ability to think on one's feet and react in new ways to different situations is indispensable. If priests are called to lead, encourage, and cooperate with others in tasks that only teams can accomplish, personal confidence and self-possession are necessary. Negative qualities are also clear. Dependent personalities should seek employment elsewhere. It is one thing too if a new generation of priests is more conservative in personal piety, but quite another if they seek to re-create Catholic parish life of the 1950s. If they do, they will shortly find themselves seriously disappointed.

Is all this aiming too high, too far over the head of the average candidate? It may be. Reality will always lower the trajectory. But it should not be the task of ideals to aim for mediocrity. The goal of the seminary might be summarized in these terms:

The seminary should strive to form a priest who is a relatively mature adult with a circle of friends. He should have an active prayer life in which he is heavily invested. He should have a grasp of Catholic doctrine and theology with basic pastoral skills. He should be enough of a self-starter to become pastor of a parish within five years of ordination. While he promises obedience to his bishop, and the promise must be taken seriously, he will be more his own boss than he may want or desire to be.

To narrow the focus even more, what can we give such a priest that will keep him on track? Certainly the kind of monitoring or support the seminary provides is out of the question. Even his own bishop does not want constant questions on matters a pastor should be able to decide for himself. Ultimately, a priest is very much on his own. The most valuable instrument we can give him at this critical juncture is a dependable interior compass to guide him in what must be a *considered* life. He needs a vision of the priesthood of Jesus Christ before his eyes and a vision of what constitutes a priestly life after the mind of Jesus Christ. The compass should help him discern where real and ideal meet. It should tell him when he is on track. It should also let him know when he fails and how badly he fails.

The remainder of this book will offer an interior compass, a vision of the priesthood of Jesus Christ and of a priestly way of life that is challenging but humane. Challenging but humane. A Protestant observer at Vatican II commented that the Decree on the Ministry and Life of Priests (1965) struck him as a *cruel* document.[8] The decree held up such relentlessly lofty ideals and sketched so little the path to their accomplishment that it could only tantalize, then frustrate the average priest. This is a great danger in the literature on spirituality and the priesthood, and surely one of the reasons why authors such as Henri Nouwen and Ronald Rolheiser have such appeal. They seem to write for actual people who are struggling to live somewhat better lives. By contrast, loftier prose seems to sail over normal heads, far beyond the range of human accomplishment. Lofty prose is also easily mouthed. Unwittingly it may contribute to a cynicism that is an old companion of clerical life. The ideals are recited. But life is lived, catch as catch can, like most human lives.

PART TWO

THE SUBJECTIVE
DONATION

Chapter Three

THE EVANGELICAL COUNSELS

P RAYER, simplicity of life, celibacy, and obedience belong together and constitute the evangelical counsels adapted to the life of the diocesan priest. Prayer is the starting point, the opening door. The counsels have never been the exclusive property of monasteries or religious life. Rather, they represent a radical vision of the Christian life and are meant to be broadly adapted to any form of living that takes the Gospel seriously. Vatican II calls them a "God-given seed" from which a "wonderful and wide-spreading tree has grown up in the field of the Lord."[1] It seems natural, then, that they would provide the structure of life for those aspiring to the priesthood and those already ordained. In this sense, they are practical topics. Of course, they can become the object of more abstract consideration, but this is not their essence or nature. They are first and foremost practical ways in which the challenge of the Gospel is taken seriously in daily life.

The evangelical counsels form points on a compass, an interior guide for priestly living. As such, they play that role because they first form the terms of a contract. They represent an agreement priests make with themselves, before Almighty God, about how they intend to live their lives. They constitute the conscious aims, and consequently the shape, priests wish to give a considered spiritual life. Prayer, simplicity, celibacy, authority, and obedience are the common forms of living for those preparing for the priesthood, which become the object of public promises made at ordination to the diaconate, repeated at ordination to the priesthood. Here metaphor becomes fact. They literally become terms of a contract that is publicly pledged and sealed before a bishop and a gathered assembly of the faithful. Then these promises look to the future. They spell out the ways priests promise they will live their lives in the years ahead.

Like any agreement that seriously binds our lives, the terms of this contract must be amended periodically. Minor adjustments are constant. When priests move, they need to seek out the right place for personal prayer, perhaps a new spiritual director or at least someone for confession. At major turning points, they may rediscover or take more seriously the life of prayer or the practice of simplicity. As their fortunes wax and wane, these practices give their lives stability and keep them on an even keel. Even in the most stable life, neglect, inattention, and laziness are problems. But so too are startling breakthroughs, moments of sheer grace, that suddenly resolve questions with which one has struggled in vain until that moment.

I will not be arguing here the theoretical merits of the counsels. My object is more modest and specific: to explain what these topics mean and how they are to be practiced, with particular focus on those first starting down the path and those who wish to take up the practice again more seriously. With topics as profound as these, everyone remains a permanent beginner. Wisdom in living is won only slowly, and all people remain recalcitrant learners until God's grace enters their lives. Here too the proof of the pudding is in the eating. The only convincing apology for the counsels is the way of life they encourage us to follow. In the final analysis, taking the challenge of the Gospel seriously is itself a large reward.

TWO GENERATIONS OF PRIESTLY SPIRITUALITY

This approach to priestly spirituality may differ from those commonly taken in the last two generations in several ways. Two generations ago, before Vatican II, priests were formed in spirituality on a diet of spiritual classics grown stale, embalmed in stately fashion in such manuals as Adolphe Tanquerey's *The Spiritual Life*.[2] Spirituality, as it appeared in manuals such as Tanquerey's, took the form of short, clear summaries of traditional positions, neatly categorized and organized. It seemed closer to a distillate of philosophical statements about the spiritual life, at best an affair of the mind, far removed from human emotion. The approach reflected at every point an almost unbridgeable dichotomy between nature and grace that led to caution, if not downright suspicion, about the role of human feeling in prayer and other spiritual practices. Such were to be *done* or *performed*, like the recitation of the breviary; it was entirely inconsequential if a substrate of human emotion accompanied them. If there was an aridity to traditional spirituality, a desiccation of once vibrant voices, this approach was largely the culprit.

Such considerations affected in every way how priests prayed before Vatican II. They said their individual masses every day with or without a congregation. They read the breviary by themselves, sometimes reverently before mass. They had a general sense of what the Latin psalms meant. Not many understood the lessons. But they read them anyway. They read the office at other times as well. It took a good hour without dawdling. When the evening news went to commercial break, priests often read the office. Sometimes, they continued when the news came back on. They took satisfaction in saying the office every day, the way a woodsman takes pride in chopping his daily quota of wood. It was also a mortal sin if they did not. That was motivation enough. It seldom occurred to a group of priests to say the office together, much less to pray spontaneously or even discuss prayer. Such were not Catholic ways.

It is understandable that in the first breezes of aggiornamento, a more human touch was called for. Human emotion demanded clearer expression. Here the efforts of Abraham Maslow and Carl Rogers were supplemented by the insights of Erik Erikson and Lawrence Kohlberg, among others. They stood ready to aid in the rehabilitation of human feeling in spirituality. And Catholics were in need of such services. In a special way, developmental psychology lent itself to spirituality (and theology) in search of human grounding. From its perspective, if human growth set the starting point, grace and human freedom provided goals, the capstone of healthy, human development. Such approaches could also claim higher validation in the anthropology of theological luminaries such as Karl Rahner.

Thus far I have disparaged the contribution of humanistic psychology because of its inability to come to terms with the reality of sin and its low estimate of the value of rules. But such weaknesses were balanced by considerable strengths. To a rule-bound tradition with a deep sense of sin like Catholicism, these approaches provided a refreshing contrast. Above all, psychology described actual human behavior in contrast to the abstract, philosophical qualities of traditional spirituality. It offered spirituality a human face. While one may critique the imbalances of developmental psychology-become-spirituality, it is not possible or desirable to reach around it and go back to the traditional spirituality of the manuals. It had the lasting benefit of making Catholic spirituality aware of its psychological conditioning, which can never be discarded or overlooked.

If there was a weakness to the marriage of spirituality and developmental psychology, it was a deeper one. All too often, starting with human development simply led to more human development. By contrast, grace and human freedom became targets that constantly receded as one approached. There were two deep truths here. First, the starting point determines everything. In this regard, can grace and human freedom be reduced to distant goals, even the capstone of healthy, human development, without unwittingly reducing spirituality, with the best of intentions, to a branch of developmental psychology? Second, in this union, apples and oranges were often mixed. In point of fact, spirituality can be joined to human nature in odd ways. What of the whiskey priests of Graham Greene and the characters of George Bernanos, François Mauriac, Flannery O'Connor, J. D. Powers, and Walker Percy among others? They seldom seemed like poster children for mental health, but they were clearly spiritual people.

THE STARTING POINT

Grace and human freedom are the starting points in our approach. This allows the incorporation of psychological insights of the past generation and avoids the reductionism. They are not only the starting point, they are as well the thread of continuity and the goal of our commonsense striving to lead a better life.

Of necessity, prayer is the first topic; simplicity, celibacy, authority, and obedience follow. They constitute the elements the candidate brings to the altar at ordination, the terms of the contract from his side, the subjective donation. What the church bestows on a candidate, the priesthood of Jesus Christ, the objective gift, will be treated in part 3. These two sides are dramatically joined at ordination. A long, often meandering education is brought to a dramatic climax, a momentous crescendo of two hours duration. The major themes are joined together in the ordination ceremony in the questions that the bishop poses about celibacy, obedience, and implicitly a certain style of life. The laying on of hands conveys the gift of the priesthood. The road ahead is set. Once ordained, priests are asked to return to these themes as they reflect on the kind of lives they lead. Are they living up to what they have promised? Are they worthy of the priesthood they received at ordination?

Priestly formation and priestly spirituality are necessarily repetitive. They address the same themes over and over again. In effect, growth in spirituality is not the same as learning more vocabulary in a foreign language or acquiring advanced techniques in computer science. The goal is vertical, not horizontal: dig the groove deeper by repeating the same themes. Indeed, one can return to these themes time and again without ever exhausting their fullness. The goal is finally connatural knowledge in which, little by little, a priest incorporates into his personal life the themes he ponders.

Regard what follows as an "overture" to priestly life, in which all the melodies that will be repeated over a lifetime are sounded together at one time. Repetition without apology. Dig the groove deeper. To seminarians, aspire in the kind of life you lead here and now to be worthy of the gift of the priesthood of Jesus Christ. When ordained, the admonition becomes simpler: *become what you are*.

TWO ADAPTATIONS

The evangelical counsels have always been regarded as broadly adaptable to Christian living. Our approach is specifically focused on diocesan priests and the challenge they face. Accordingly, two adaptations of the counsels have been made to keep the discussion as close as possible to actual diocesan priestly life. Diocesan priests do not take vows of poverty. Simplicity of life is a broadly derived term that asks priests to examine their lives as a whole. My assumption is that the greatest possessions that offend against authentic Christian living are spiritual, not material, in nature. In the long run, a priest's fixed ideas and, above all, his sins are the burdens and possessions that weigh him down. Therefore while it may be regrettable that diocesan priests sometimes become worldly collectors of eccentric items, from Waterford crystal to electric trains, such are a symptom, not the cause of a priestly life run amok. The second adaptation regards the issue of authority. Father Raymond E. Brown, S.S., renowned biblical scholar, was also an astute observer of diocesan priestly life. His view, repeated often to me at St. Patrick's Seminary in Menlo Park, California, was that the use of authority posed a greater challenge to diocesan priests than the practice of obedience. If the abuse of authority is a vice, then its right exercise is a virtue. These were wise words. In this day, when priests become pastors so quickly, when collaborative ministry flourishes, the right exercise of authority must be regarded as a high virtue that diocesan priests must consciously cultivate.

Chapter Four

PRAYER

PRAYER IS THE STARTING POINT because our first assumption
is that priests cannot lead the life of the evangelical counsels
by virtue of their own strength and surely not as the result of a
supercharged act of will. It is God's life within us that gives us the
strength and perspective to follow the Gospel more faithfully. Those
who do not wish to take the life of prayer seriously should not aspire
to the life of counsels. If they do, they will only find frustration and
soon abandon the effort as one more case of failed self-help. Prayer
must be the beginning, middle, and end, for it provides priests with
a fixed point of reference, a knowledge of where true north lies in
the journey ahead.

THE LITURGY AND THE EUCHARIST

A distinction must be drawn between personal prayer in all its
forms and the official prayer, the *worship* of the church. The prayer
of the church, preeminently the liturgy of the Eucharist, is the great
act of worship that Christ, the Son of God, offers to God the Father
in and through the Holy Spirit. Priest and people as members of
the Body of Christ take part in and are carried along by the Son's
worship of the Father.

This great act of thanksgiving establishes the frame of reference
for all forms of prayer and Christians should endeavor to keep this
fact in mind. This is no small challenge. The thought is so large and
human minds so modest that one can consciously understand only
a fragment of its meaning. The air grows thin and the lungs gasp
for oxygen as they seek to grasp a thought of such lofty elevation.
Even the most dutiful consciousness finds its attention span further
eroded by simple habit. People participate in the liturgy on a regular

basis. It becomes of necessity a ritual in which they take part with varying degrees of awareness and concentration.

For many reasons, a *human* reference point is needed in order to understand how one should relate to the *divine* action of the liturgy. Vatican II's Constitution on the Liturgy provides a starting point. It enjoins on all the faithful as a first duty "full, conscious, and active participation in liturgical celebrations which is demanded by the very nature of the liturgy."[1] This injunction sets the bar high: Christians must prepare themselves carefully to participate in the Eucharist with all the concentration and attention that the liturgy deserves. They need to be recollected, attentive, and composed in order to be active, conscious participants. But the injunction also assumes that just as they are inserted into a mystery far beyond their comprehension, so too they respond to it in ways far beyond reflective awareness. Christians resonate on conscious and unconscious levels to the mystery of God's presence that surrounds and engulfs them. In other words, while the first duty is "full, conscious, and active participation," this does not circumscribe the total range of response.

Han Urs von Balthasar offers a family of helpful images, "a sounding box," "an aeolian harp," that describe how the human person is attuned to God.[2] They suggest that the human spirit resonates on multiple levels to the mystery of God's presence the way a tuning fork reverberates to sound. In one sense, consciousness would be seriously overburdened if Christians tried to keep continually before their eyes the nature of the mystery that surrounds them. The light is simply too dazzling and human want of perception often has a self-protective tinge. But Christians are reminded that if they are inserted in the great prayer of the Trinity in a way far beyond normal, human reckoning, the only adequate response is to insert that mystery into the center of their lives.

Therefore the church's liturgy has a unique capacity to act as a metronome, setting the rhythm of human life beyond normal human appreciation or understanding. This is the reason why people attend mass regularly and follow the liturgical year. It gives direction to their lives. In this sense, if they are enjoined to "full, active, conscious participation" as their first duty, they are also called simply to "be there," to attend in varying moods with different degrees of conscious awareness, sure in the knowledge that the liturgy works in them in multiple ways. The *divine* action of the liturgy gives a sense of orientation to very *human* lives. This is its first and deepest gift.

Some practical thoughts are in order here. If the liturgy belongs first to the church, this means it belongs first to the worshiping community. For if the liturgy gives Christians individually a sense of orientation, it does this by rightly orienting the community in which they pray. From this perspective, prayer as an isolated endeavor is a rare and unnatural thing. This communal orientation of prayer also cuts against the individualism of the age, and the clash is everywhere evident. There is, for example, an almost automatic tendency to want to adjust the community's liturgy to one's individual taste. If the liturgy is a living prayer, it will also differ somewhat from parish to parish, perhaps from region to region. A new community always takes some getting used to. What gestures does the community make together? Do they raise their hands at the Our Father? When do they kneel and when do they stand? In liturgy, it is always small differences that become major annoyances.

The rule of thumb here is twofold. The individual adapts to the community, not vice versa, and the fit is never perfect. With some effort, people eventually become accustomed to different habits in a new community. In the process, they are reminded that liturgy, like all forms of ritual, comprises small habits that are performed without much conscious thought. There are also important lessons here for those who preside at the liturgy. If the liturgy belongs to no one in particular, the presider must exemplify this impartiality. A hard-won lesson of the first generation of liturgical reforms is that there are ways of presiding at the Eucharist that obstruct and obscure the nature of the liturgy. This is the prayer of the church, and it should be celebrated in a personal but neutral way so that the congregation has a sense that their right to "full, active, and conscious participation" is respected. The words of the canon "We your people and your ministers" contain an implicit injunction to the

celebrant: pray the words that follow in a way that invites the worshiping community to enter into this great prayer of thanksgiving
offered to God in their name.

The liturgy structures the life of the community in which it is
celebrated and gives it its first and proudest title: a community of
prayer to the Father through the Son in the Spirit. The communal
prayer of the church provides the seedbed in which a personal life
of prayer can grow and flourish.

PERSONAL PRAYER

Personal prayer is different. If the liturgy belongs first to the community, habits of personal prayer belong to the individual. They
need to be tailored to the person the way a well-worn glove fits the
hand; the fit must be snug, comfortable, and easy. This only comes
with time.

All forms of prayer assume that the human person is a creature of many levels, conscious and unconscious. The image of the
tuning fork is helpful not only in describing the various ways in
which Christians respond to God's presence but also the multiple
ways in which they themselves pray. They recite the rosary aloud
or to themselves while at another level, beneath the words, they
contemplate the mysteries of Christ's life. At other times, they talk
to Christ as they might converse with a good friend. They con-
sult the Lord about their plans, seek his guidance at crucial times,
and share with him their thoughts as Christians always have. The
"You" to whom St. Augustine's famed *Confessions* were directed
so long ago is the same Lord God with whom Christians converse
today. Often they may fall silent, as Fenelon writes, as we might
with a good friend with whom for the moment all words have been
exhausted and we are content to simply sit quietly together.[3] At
other times, they pray in wordless adoration at the presence of God
that surrounds them on every side, closer to them than they are to
themselves. Finally, it is God's spirit at the deepest level that not
only teaches us to pray but prays in us. In a modest and personal
way, Christians duplicate in their own lives the great movement of

the church's liturgy. God's spirit prays in them, returning to God the worship of the Son in the Spirit.

If Christians pray in multiple ways, they are in the last analysis brought back to a single truth. Luther's description of the human person outside grace, *homo in se incurvatus*, the creature turned in on itself, is not only a reminder of our unique capacity for inner awareness, but equally that the final trajectory of this inward curve is outward.[4] If humans are built to be reflective creatures, they are even more deeply constructed to turn to God in prayer. This is the difference between prayer and introspection. Introspection is sometimes helpful but just as often a disappointing, frustrating exercise. The arc of consciousness is not completed. Continuing the arc to its resting place, prayer by contrast is invariably the bearer of rich gifts of peace, strength, courage, joy, and insight. This truth underscores a single fact. The goal of the human spirit, the aim of its trajectory, is the Lord God. This is our deepest intuition and a true one, and the reason why Christians rest so content when they discover it personally and individually.

For all these reasons, prayer is a simple yet complex undertaking. Prayer is a garment of folds and layers that must conform to the shape of an individual's personality. Because of the complexity of the undertaking, the help of another in developing habits of prayer, especially in the beginning stages, is vital. The process takes time and cannot be rushed. Likewise it calls for the "discernment of spirits." Not all movements of the spirit take us in the right direction. This is so because, though the Holy Spirit dwells within us, the human heart also shares its abode with less worthy spirits and baser instincts.

Since the impulse to pray follows closely the contours of the human spirit, prayer is an eminently practical topic, the source of traditional wisdom and time-honored advice. For those beginning to set down the keel of a personal prayer life, it is better to pray on a daily basis for a modest period of time, say twenty minutes, than to pray sporadically for long stretches. The same advice applies to those renewing habits of prayer that have fallen into desuetude. Prayer is a daily habit that is best begun in small stretches and then extended. Often books on prayer, especially traditional ones, were written *by* introverts *for* other introverts, those who could sit quietly in one spot for an extended period. To the extrovert who wanders down this path, beware! Traditional advice often does not fit more outgoing personalities who need to be active in prayer, and adjustments should be made accordingly.

Lastly, God deserves the choicest portion of the day. For some that may be early morning, for others late evening. There is no preferred time. The right place for personal prayer is also important, whether it's a study, a chapel, or outdoors.

People need the help of a spiritual director in answering the many questions, practical and personal, that are part of developing a life of prayer. They also need discipline and willpower in prayer; but these are like auxiliary engines on a sailboat. They are meant to maneuver us out of the harbor and into the wind. Then the wind must fill our sails. That wind is the presence of God's spirit in the life of prayer, and that means that prayer must ultimately become a joy, not a duty.

THE LITURGY OF THE HOURS

The Liturgy of the Hours belongs to the official prayer of the church, and priests and deacons are obliged to recite it on a daily basis, the age-old custom and practice of the church that hallows the hours of the day with moments of prayer. The present Liturgy of the Hours represents an enormous improvement over the old breviary. In less than a generation, the stale recitation of the Latin breviary in fulfillment of a canonical obligation has been transformed into a genuine source of prayer and reflection, not just for priests, deacons, and religious but for all Christians who wish to give themselves more fully to a life of prayer. The treasury of the Scriptures and classic spiritual writing has been opened up and made accessible for a new generation. The rules governing the recitation have also been formulated, first, to invite and encourage prayer and, in that light, to oblige its recitation.[5]

The Liturgy of the Hours occupies for most seminarians and priests a midway position between personal prayer and public liturgy. This is so because of the various ways in which it is prayed. It is recited in common with different degrees of solemnity. It is also recited individually and privately. Most seminaries encourage individual recitation because this is the usual way diocesan priests pray the Liturgy of the Hours after ordination.

When the church entrusts the Liturgy of the Hours to young seminarians and religious, it gives young men and women a very large pair of shoes. The psalms in particular far exceed the normal range of emotions that Christians feel themselves capable of experiencing, much less actually expressing in prayer. Indeed, they represent a veritable calliope of feelings in which almost every conceivable human emotion is sounded, and, were the psalms not so honored, we would flee from the direct way in which guilt, despair, and exaltation are expressed. Consider Psalm 51, recited at Morning Prayer each Friday.

> Have mercy on me, God,
>   according to your steadfast love;
> according to your abundant mercy
>   blot out my transgressions.
> Wash me thoroughly from my iniquity,
>   and cleanse me from my sin.
> For I know my transgressions,
>   and my sin is ever before me. . . .
> Indeed, I was born guilty,
>   a sinner when my mother conceived me.
>   (vv. 1–3, 5)

The haunting lament of Psalm 137 (Evening Prayer on Tuesday of Week IV) still echoes the sad cadence of Israel's exile, its sense of loss and mourning:

> By the rivers of Babylon —
>   there we sat down and there we wept
>   when we remembered Zion.
> On the willows there
>   we hung up our harps.

> For there our captors
>   asked us for songs,
> and our tormentors asked for mirth saying,
>   "Sing us one of the songs of Zion."
> How could we sing the LORD's song
>   in a foreign land?
> If I forget you, O Jerusalem,
>   let my right hand wither!" (vv. 1–5)

A protective mechanism bids us not to examine such passages too closely. But in frank expression of religious feeling, the psalms are unsurpassed. Only with age does one grow into a recitation deserving of their eloquence and depth.

Because of the nature of the psalms and of public prayer itself, the recitation of the Liturgy of the Hours in common will vary widely, and there is a virtue to each variation. Morning Prayer may be recited in a rushed way as an obligation discharged without much thought. But "being there" for the plain recitation of the Liturgy of the Hours even without much spirit is not without its virtue. The tuning fork may not stir much but at least it is upright.

POWERFUL PRAYER

From time to time the inherent power of the psalms captures the hearts of those who recite them so that, for a short while, the prayer takes off and becomes a conflagration of praise to the Lord in which the worshipers are deserving of their inspired words. And it was always so. I recall as a young seminarian stealing into the chapel of a monastery for the recitation of compline. Since many of the monks knew the prayer by heart, they turned off the reading light above their choir stalls. As they recited the office, the staid and formal prayer suddenly seemed to catch fire as their voices lifted. The ancient sentiments of Israel's prayer were met and matched by the feelings of these monks more than two millennia later. One tangibly understood at that moment the power of a living tradition of prayer.

BY THEIR FRUITS

All movements of the spirit, and all forms of prayer, are measured by their fruits. "You will know them by their fruits," says Matthew's Gospel. Prayer is far too deep, mysterious, and personal to attest to its authenticity on its own. From the stories of the Gospels down to Molière's *Tartuffe,* there is a long tradition of the pious fraud for whom prayer and devotion are an elaborate ruse behind which baser instincts hide. There is no reason to think this shadow tradition flags today.

What are the fruits of prayer that attest to and certify their interior truth and validity? Surely the forgiveness of sin and peace in the heart would rank high on the list. The first encounters of the risen Jesus with his followers were experiences in which he forgave their infidelities. John's Gospel relates the words of Jesus to his disciples, cowering behind closed doors, "Peace be with you. As the Father has sent me, even so I send you. And when he had said this, he breathed on them and said to them, 'Receive the Holy Spirit. If you forgive the sins of any, they are forgiven; if you retain the sins of any, they are retained'" (John 20:19, 21–22). Peace and forgiveness are the first gifts of the risen Lord. The forgiveness of others is inseparable from the forgiveness of self, the last and perhaps most difficult link in the chain. These fruits show themselves as a life of charity in word and deed, the complement of a genuine life of prayer. It is hard to imagine a true spirit of prayer resting in an ungenerous heart.

Ernst Käsemann wrote a small book many years ago entitled *Jesus Means Freedom.*[6] The title touches another manifestation of the power of prayer. Jesus not only forgave sins; he cast out demons and evil spirits who held the human spirit in thrall. The demons of old, hale and hearty creatures, are nothing if not adaptable. They are alive and well today, transforming themselves easily in the modern world, dressed now in new attire. They appear among us as the addiction to drugs, alcohol, and other substances that entrap the human spirit. The addictions to power, rank, and ambition need little adaptation and remain the same as they always were, with their adoration of false gods who enslave and disfigure

the human spirit. It is surely significant that "twelve-step" programs that potently combat various forms of addiction depend on
the acknowledgment of human helplessness and the existence of
a "higher power." Christians give this instinct definition and say,
in Käsemann's words, "Jesus means freedom." The true presence
of God in prayer is a liberating one that frees us from bonds and
shackles of every kind, from the dross of old habit to the addiction
to drugs and alcohol. Jesus also frees us from false gods so that we
might serve the true God.

But perhaps the most enduring way in which the power of prayer
manifests itself is as a source of strength that goes beyond normal powers and capacities. This is what William James observed,
and this capacity remains an accurate gauge of the power of prayer,
indeed, of religious faith.[7] Religious experience, above all prayer,
gives people an inner resource they can tap at critical moments.
Equally important is a sense of perspective. Prayer sheds light and
perspective on all aspects of human life.

In the life of the counsels, prayer provides a sense of true north,
our first point of reference. But it also gives strength, courage, and
endurance, not just compass, but motor too. These elements come
together in simplicity of life.

Chapter Five

THE CHALLENGE OF SIMPLICITY OF LIFE

PRAYER AND SIMPLICITY OF LIFE

I F PRAYER is what Christians do for a certain number of minutes a day, say twenty minutes or an hour, simplicity is what they do with the rest of the time. In other words, simplicity of life addresses the topic of how the presence of God in prayer permeates life as a whole, shaping the way people live and conduct their affairs. Moments of prayer are the ordering metronomes that set the basic rhythm of life. They do so because they provide the gifts that grace alone can bring: a sense of purpose and a special source of strength. In prayer, Christians seek a sense of direction that gives perspective to their entire lives. Through prayer, they gain the strength to do their duty and sometimes to do extraordinary things in which they surprise themselves.

The Lord's injunction to his disciples is the essence of simplicity. "He ordered them to take nothing for their journey except a staff; no bread, no bag, no money in their belts; but to wear sandals and not put on two tunics" (Mark 6:8–9). Jesus tells his disciples what *not* to take. He does not tell them what to do. No surprise for the Jesus who sharpens the Torah in the antitheses of the Sermon on the Mount, who sums up the law in two commandments, love of God and love of neighbor. Jesus depends on the disciples' interior motivation, the spirit of God dwelling in them and their own focus on the kingdom, the point of their mission. The rest takes care of itself.

Our topic breaks down into two asymmetrical parts. Simplicity of life as an object of reflection remains ever elusive, the object of only occasional sighting and often a matter of conjecture even to oneself. Simplicity as a practical topic on the other hand — how to actually lead a simple life — is as clear, direct, and difficult as the first part is mysterious. Here the difficulty quickly becomes, *Can I do it?* These parts come together in the discussion of sin and simplicity of life: how the burden of sin affects the capacity to lead a simple life.

SIMPLICITY OF LIFE
AS AN OBJECT OF REFLECTION

Simplicity of life, poverty, is usually reckoned the first of the evangelical counsels. It looks to life as a whole and enjoys the pre-eminence of the whole over the parts. Celibacy and obedience are more focused in the challenge they pose, and that underscores the problem of simplicity. Life as a whole? How does the mind encompass such a vast topic? It is a bit like hugging an elephant. Perhaps praiseworthy in intention but not so easily accomplished. For this reason, simplicity of life is a worthy and fruitful topic of reflection that is never exhausted. The plain fact is that most people discover the larger complexion of their lives only in hindsight and indirectly in those rare moments when they are forced to make hard choices about what matters to them. Such choices provide privileged glimpses into personal character.

CHOICES

A woman lived in a great house in Dresden during the middle stages of the Cold War when it was possible but still dangerous to cross the border from East to West Germany. Her children had already preceded her to the West. When the time came for her to follow, she was given one hour's notice and told she could bring only one suitcase. What to take from this vast house in which her family had lived for generations? She took the following items. A silver comb and brush set that belonged to her mother, two books her husband had written, which were in his judgment, his best. As many family photographs as she could find. She paused before she mentioned

*the last item. "I took lots of clean underwear," she said. "I could
not imagine beginning a new life without clean underwear." These
choices constitute precise brush strokes in a portrait of a practical
woman beginning life anew in her middle years.*

The vignette is instructive for several reasons. A sense of life as
a whole remains elusive. Its existence is presumed in legal documents, in wills, birth certificates, passports, and the like. The
presumption is even larger when lifetime commitments are made
at marriage or ordination. But at any one moment, people *experience* its presence only indirectly. What burdens or encumbers
them at any one time may deliver a downward tug on life as a
whole. The spirit sags. At joyous moments, on the other hand, all
life seems to lift. They float higher in the water. As an object of
reflection, the shape of life as a whole appears only in rare or extraordinary moments of decision like the woman fleeing Dresden
with a single suitcase containing her treasures. The hard decisions are what prompts the clear sighting of the whole through
its particular parts.

When these clues are assembled, how do they describe the object of reflection? The human person seems to resemble a funnel.
On one end, wide and open-ended. Life is comprised of a series of
roles to be played (wife, husband, son, daughter); *activities* under-
taken (in business, travel, recreation); *other persons* from whose
lives one's own life is barely separable (spouse, children, parents,
friends); and *places* where a person belongs (homes, apartments,
summer houses). The sense of self, William James observed, ex-
tends to our clothes, our horses, and our bank accounts, so widely
does the net of personal concern extend.[1]

Yet these roles, activities, persons, and places are finally threaded
through a very narrow eye of a needle. They are held together by a
sense of self that can be variously represented. James described its
movement as a stream of consciousness; Pascal, more reflectively,
as a thinking reed between time and eternity. But however one describes it, a single, central axis holds together many things if they
are held together at all. Finally, people die one by one. As the spirit
returns to God, worldly activities cease, consigned to the memories

of others or preserved in accomplishments that outlast the span of one's years.

James's description of the self moves the question forward, suggesting a dynamic quality to what might otherwise remain a static description. It underscores a central truth that might be overlooked but that, once acknowledged, transforms the discussion: simplicity of life is a moving virtue. A sense of life as a whole is not a permanent but a temporary possession, lost and found many times in the course of a lifetime. The core might aptly be described as a course to be followed as people race through a series of unavoidable rapids. They marry, divorce, have children, get sick, move, change jobs, retire. They lose a parent, a child, friends, a job. In the course of these events, they inevitably lose their way. They can't always maintain flank speed or keep ahead of the current. They drift. Parts of life float off by themselves. Simplicity of life is lost.

On the other hand, when life seems to "work," people have a sense of direction or purpose. The motor starts, and the tugboat moves along. What might have been described as a scattered amalgam of pieces, parts, and episodes comes together in a complex ordered whole again. The tugboat is now pushing a line of barges securely held together, moving in a single direction. This is how the presence of God works in human life. While believers play diverse roles, engage in different activities, are attached to many people and places, while they encounter difficulties and challenges along the way, the presence of God establishes a set of priorities, creating a sense of order in their life as a whole. A single shape emerges. Simplicity of life is won. It should be clear that a simple life does not exclude enormous complexity. On the contrary, what human life is not complex? The difference is that in a simple life, the center holds. The center is where God dwells.

God's presence, however, is not static but dynamic. We should then speak more directly of God's Providence, acting and guiding the course of human life. Like the first disciples, we ask, What is God calling me to do? What is my mission? The notion of God's Providence that writes in neon lights and capital letters, giving generic directions to the human family, is not very believable. Providence must write first in the fine print, in the tiniest details of a single human life, in the parts of the human equation that are most complex. The more one learns about genetic coding, for example, the more it becomes clear that human genes are not third-class mail, delivering generally helpful advice about health and human hygiene. On the contrary, they are enormously complex, detailed game plans for single individuals. How much more complex must be the working of God's Providence, not least of all because it must encompass the domain of human freedom?

Believers never can have a simple, clear picture of their lives delivered to their consciousness no matter now much they reflect or meditate. No single picture is available this side of eternity because as long as we draw breath, life remains a work in progress. The best hope is for a series of angled shots of a moving target. One person's life is inextricably connected to the free decisions of other people, which cannot be foreseen or predicted. Further, chance accidents occur, mishaps that come out of nowhere. In fact, the desire for too much clarity is generally counted as a fault. The impulse to control the free flow of life can only have the unfortunate effect of making people more constrained in a game best played with a loose hand. Here Søren Kierkegaard's advice is wise indeed: If you want to cut much wood, do not press too hard on the saw, for then the saw will bind and you will cut no wood at all.[2]

However, a sense of life as a whole remains the object of a person's shrewdest intuition and surely worthy of reflection from time to time, perhaps on a yearly retreat. What does my life as a whole resemble at this point? Only moving comparisons are helpful. Life might be fairly compared to a series of card games in which people play the hand they were dealt with greater or lesser skill. It does not pay to get too far ahead because no one is sure how others will play their cards. Still, most players have some sense of where the game stands. Have they played their face cards? Have they made serious mistakes, been out-trumped when they should have ducked? Are they left with only the remnants of a hand, a two of spades and a three of diamonds? Often human intuition is on the money. It amazed me as a young priest to hear older people in confession calmly announce that their bags were packed and they were ready to die. In effect, they had played their hand almost to the end and were quite aware of the fact.

Another image of Kierkegaard's captures a side of the picture. "One who rows a boat turns his back to the goal toward which he labors."[3] People live forward but think backward. They are never exactly sure where they are going, only where they have been. But that is to know much. Sometimes in retrospect, they can trace with almost surgical precision the careful line God's Providence has drawn in the unexpected twists and turns of their lives, inexorably moving toward a single purpose that only slowly comes to clear consciousness. When it does, a sense of wonder, puzzlement, and awe mingle. The Portuguese proverb comes to mind: "God writes straight with crooked lines."

GOD'S PROVIDENCE

Matthew's genealogy is worth pondering. Who would have guessed the seed of the Messiah was slumbering in so many strange breasts, in the best and worst of Israel's kings, in David, Solomon, and Josiah, but in Manasseh and Jechoniah as well? The seed of the Messiah passed directly through the nadir of the Israelite monarchy. One of the women in the genealogy, Rahab, was a prostitute. And what of the nameless, anonymous Jews after the exile? Who could imagine a line as crooked and zigzagged as the one that the genealogy draws?

Such lines continue to be drawn and in the strangest of places. A woman in Marin Country, just north of San Francisco, experienced a recurrence of breast cancer when she was in her mid-forties. By any reckoning, her life was in shambles. Her husband, long jobless, had been consigned to a room in the basement. Two teenage sons thankfully exhausted themselves daily in sports. But a daughter, on the verge of her teens, was her mother's worst nightmare. All the truculent genes of many generations of strong, Irish women seemed to converge on this one twelve-year-old.

The woman decided to go to Lourdes to seek a cure. She borrowed money from her mother for the trip. After the usual stay, she returned home to Marin County. She died of breast cancer about a year later. A usually voluble woman, she never talked about her visit to Lourdes. But it was clear in the year that was left to her that she had learned something. Shortly after she returned, she moved her husband out of the basement. She seemed to grasp that her death, which would normally fragment a family already badly splintered, had to be made into the glue that held them together. She never said this to anyone, but in retrospect, it was undoubtedly her plan. Did she get this intuition at Lourdes or on the way home on the plane? God knows. But she managed to bring her family together in the act of her own death. The selfless generosity of a dying woman finally melted the strong will of her daughter, just turned thirteen. When she was sure the glue was holding, she died. And her family has continued to grow as she would have wanted. Five years later, the center has held. There is an ancient tradition about the ars moriendi, *the art of dying. Somewhere, somehow God's Providence taught this woman that art, and she brought her family together around it. God writes straight with crooked lines. Even in Marin County.*

SIMPLICITY OF LIFE
IN SEMINARY FORMATION

While simplicity of life as an object of reflection remains ever elusive, the practice of simplicity is different. Here the basic rules for simple living are themselves simple. In many ways, that is the heart of the problem. The demands they place are so clear and unrelenting that they allow little room for evasive maneuver and no place to hide. The question quickly becomes, Can I do it? Those who manage to lead a simple life also follow roughly the same path; if the road is simple, it is also straight, steep, and difficult.

The subject of simplicity of life must be a special source of reflection in seminary formation. Simplicity of life is practiced with relative ease in the seminary. The goal of the program is clear, preparation for the Roman Catholic priesthood. Those who do not share that goal quickly leave. Even the obstacles whet the appetite. A long, detailed course of studies and a daily schedule of prayer give a reliable sense of direction and progress; they provide sheltering wings. Living in a single room is itself an exercise in simplicity of life. It also guarantees privacy and protective anonymity.

Most of these supports disappear with ordination. If simplicity is easily practiced in the seminary, it is usually the first virtue lost after ordination. A newly ordained priest is pulled in multiple directions by public demands, on the one hand, as he is deprived of privacy and anonymity on the other. A sense of life as a whole disappears into a series of other-directed tasks. His life is not his own. The priesthood as a future ideal toward which one has been striving for many years also appears in a different light when it becomes a present possession. The image may not be elegant but it is accurate. At times, newly ordained priests resemble plucked chickens.

These factors should be carefully considered in seminary formation because the forces that cause this outward motion can only increase. Given the age and scarcity of clergy, the public demands on priests will grow. Hence an even firmer sense of personal discipline will be demanded of young priests in the future. Such personal self-discipline will have many components. The following four maxims provide important starting points. They are very specific in accordance with the difficulties newly ordained priests face.

Maxim One: Take care of your physical health. For all: develop regular habits of exercise *now* and keep in reasonable physical condition. For some: stop smoking. For others: lose weight. At the very least, get in the habit of some form of daily exercise, if only a long walk every day. This rule grows out of long experience. If, for example, young men are overweight in the seminary, they usually become humongous after ordination. The number of overweight seminarians who lost weight after ordination could hold a national convention in a phone booth. The rule of thumb leads in the opposite direction. If a seminarian neglects his physical health now, the problem only grows worse later. Then he will be forced to devote more, not less time to his physical well-being. He will complicate, not simplify, his life.

As the multiple demands of public ministry descend on a young man, he invariably heads in one of two directions. Either he develops habits of regular exercise, reducing tension in a healthy and productive way, or he begins to overeat, the most common compensatory behavior to which priests are drawn. The flight is to food, safe, available balm for daily frustration. The deleterious effects of smoking as well as the powerfully addictive hold it exercises are well known. It remains a very costly compensatory behavior, an even more illusory enjoyment. Seminaries should firmly direct young men to stop smoking, as they direct advanced smokers toward formal programs for withdrawal.

The logic of this first maxim, as difficult as it may be in practice, is abundantly clear. If physical health is neglected, life becomes less simple and more complex. Hence in seminary formation, one set of habits should be firmly encouraged (exercise, proper diet, moderation in drinking) and another set should be discouraged (smoking, overeating, and immoderate drinking). The increased stress of priestly ministry reinforces bad habits already in place, and reversing those habits in an even more stressful environment is twice as difficult.

Maxim Two: Go to confession regularly. This is a matter of spiritual health and of practicing what one preaches. If priests encourage Catholics to go to confession, they should go themselves on a regular basis. While priests are regularly advised to seek a spiritual director, the plain fact is that it is not easy to find one. But a priest can find someone for regular confession.

The sacrament of Reconciliation is itself in the process of recovery after a generation of upheaval and some neglect. Priests will need to preach about the importance of Christ's reconciliation, present in the sacrament. Some priests, like some Catholics, may have fallen out of the habit of regular confession. And probably for the same reasons. It is painful, difficult, and embarrassing to confess one's sins, not least of all because they remain so much the same. Most people make almost the same confession every time. That itself constitutes a humbling acknowledgment of their dependence on God's grace to help them where their own strength falters. They must also learn to wait with patience for such grace to arrive. No one can control God's end of the equation. Not only is it a humbling matter of personal integrity for priests and seminarians but important for ministers and future ministers of the sacrament.

Maxim Three: Make sure there is a fit between public task and personal energy. People are variously endowed with energy, talent, and imagination. Some seem to have small, compact engines that work best with manageable jobs. Others require large, demanding tasks for smooth running. When they are underemployed, they quickly become victims of their own imagination and unused energy. Indeed, a complex and demanding public task is often the key to a simple life, providing an outlet for abundant talent, energy and imagination. It is a stroke of good fortune to have a public task that fits an individual's personality. It is also true wisdom to have a sense of the size and scope of one's own spirit and ambition and the public tasks that correspond to them. It is well within the bounds of obedience to seek an assignment that corresponds to one's level of talent, energy, intelligence, and imagination. It is obvious that when people are fully engaged and their mind has a steady focus, they settle down and their lives invariably become simpler.

Maxim Four: Let prayer take the place of imagination. Imagination is the faculty that allows people to project beyond their present situation and see themselves creatively transported to a variety of different places. It explores the best and worst of potential situations as they begin to unfold. Empathy and pity transport people to the plight of those less fortunate than themselves. In worry, imagination explores the dark potential of a new situation. The doctor notices a blemish. Imagination sees a melanoma. Indeed, worry often has people crossing complex, imaginary bridges two or three times when the actual bridge they must cross spans another river.

Let prayer take the place and do the work of imagination. Pray about large concerns beyond your control. Worry about small things within your control. This maxim only works if we have enough confidence in the power of prayer to let the unknown future with all its possibilities rest in God's hands and carry us beyond our own resources. A good example here is the matter of a priestly vocation. This should be the object of prayer. Worry about such a large and important topic quickly becomes a circular exercise in which a young man is finally talking to himself. "Do or don't I have a vocation? Is my old job open? Where will I live?" Far better to pray, "Lord, give me light about my vocation. Give me light about the path ahead, which is dark to me now." If one prays daily with confidence, in God's time the answer will drop into one's lap. This is how prayer works.

The logic as well as the difficulty of the maxim is clear. Prayer should be directed toward those large concerns that are beyond one's normal strength and imagining. Those objects are truly worthy of prayer. But the first inclination of everyone is to worry. The slightest reflection, however, reveals how little worry actually helps, indeed how much it adds to the burden. Past experience allows us to let prayer take the lead. In other words, confidence in the power of prayer is developed as we witness how, time after time, prayer carries us beyond our own strength and imagining. But the first step each time, to place confidence first in prayer, is never easy.

SIN AND SIMPLICITY OF LIFE

The two aspects of the discussion on the reflection about and the practice of simplicity of life come together in the questions of how the burden of sin affects the desire to lead a simple life. On the side of reflection, the knowledge of personal sin is as hidden and inscrutable as any aspect of life. On the side of practice, the decision to seek forgiveness or to offer it to others is often arduous and difficult and fully shares the hard challenge of the practical maxims. They come together here because the subject of sin so fully engages all aspects of the human person.

In the last analysis, the major burdens that encumber and impede a simple life are the wounds inflicted by others and the sins people themselves commit. Clearly all people bear wounds that need healing. The scars of childhood have an inevitable way of lingering. Adult experience only adds to the catalogue of hurts. In this regard, people suffer innocently, the victims of another's ill will or of an adverse turn of fortune. Old wounds also tie people to the past, to the incidents that caused them in the first place. In addition, people not only grow accustomed to but attached to old hurts.

In an otherwise uneventful life, an old wound may become a source of present meaning. Victims thus become cooperators in their own misery.

Personal sin represents the more active side of the equation, the side in which people are not victims but perpetrators in varying degrees either by commission, omission, or cooperation. One way or another, others suffer innocently at their hands. In this regard, they seek the pardon of Almighty God and the forgiveness of those they have injured.

Knowledge of Sins

But old difficulties return with a vengeance on both scores. It is not easy to know one's own sins. Sin goes to the bone; an accurate knowledge of personal sin is tantamount to an accurate knowledge of oneself, and who is sure here? Most of us are far too compromised, far too prone to fool ourselves. Knowing one's sins is a simple but herculean human accomplishment and a great grace as well. These abstract notions become clearer when we bring them closer to actual life.

KNOWING OUR SINS

"I had another letter from Sister Grace Kleppner in Sioux Falls, Iowa, thanking me for my recent article in the Catholic Register. *She circulated a series of my articles in her community. They found them very helpful and would like me to come out to speak." This is an example of the steady diet of plaudits recounted by a man to his colleagues at 5:30 almost every evening. The fan letters seemed mostly to come from religious women with German surnames, a large portion, like Sister Grace, from Iowa. It was a lot to put up with at the end of the day. After a while, when a new batch of letters was unveiled, the colleagues would just look at one another and roll their eyes. The man never noticed that his colleagues were, in effect, laughing at him behind his back. So it went for a long time.*

Then one day, one of the colleagues thought, "I wonder if people do the same thing to me? I wonder if they roll their eyes behind my back?" As soon as he posed the question, he knew the answer was . . . yes. People were probably doing it right now, although it seemed impossible in his case. How much do we really know ourselves? he wondered. How much do we know our sins? He thought of two friends. One saw himself as "courageously straightforward, even when it hurts." Others regarded him as a man with a vicious tongue and a mean streak. The other fancied himself "consistently principled in action." Others thought he was stubborn as a goat.

How well do people know themselves? How well do they know their sins? No one is sure. Probably not well at all. Evil is always chosen under the aspect of good, and a cloud of self-deception hangs over each person's head. But if a cloud covers one's own eyes, it does not extend to others. Most of the time, their perceptions ring true. The sure sign of "secret faults" in one's life, wrote Cardinal Newman, is the public presence of such faults in the lives of others, oblivious to them but plain for all the world to see.[4] This converges on a single point: it is a great grace to know one's sins, a grace for which Christians daily pray and one that can never be presumed.

Sorrow for Sin

It is an equally great grace to feel sorrow or compunction for one's sins. People always know what makes them *feel* bad. But it is not always clear that their *sins* make them feel bad. And some of the things that do, snacking between meals, coming late for an appointment, are not really sins. Often one blithely undertakes actions that grievously wound others without so much as a second thought. In these cases, self-deception conspires with willfulness. For sin is an action, a decision that sets the ball rolling in one direction. Repentance must stop the forward movement and reverse the course. It is literally a matter of metanoia, of changing one's mind and heart, and then one's action. Sorrow for sin often takes the form of an apology, but it is hard to stop a sinful act, hard to reverse course, and very hard to acknowledge the reversal consciously. It is not only a great grace to repent of one's sins but an act of human courage as well.

REPENTANCE

Two sisters in their mid-seventies had been alienated for thirty years. They lived across the street from one another. Their relatives called the street the DMZ. The sisters could observe one another's daily habits, which day each one shopped, went to the bank, went to church. Relatives tried to piece together how the fight, began but no one was sure. A cousin thought that if one sister visited the other and offered an apology, an old fight might be over in a trice. Sure, his brother countered, but there was a snowball's chance in hell that would happen. But, in fact, he was wrong. Each sister had thought of crossing the DMZ. One had made it halfway across the street, and then her courage faltered. So as presidents came and went, as the Berlin Wall fell, the animosity between these sisters remained.

Then one of them suddenly died. The family thought the other might rejoice at having outlived her enemy. Instead, she became deeply disoriented. The animosity between them had been a linch-pin of her life, and though it continued after death, it was easier to dislike a living person than a memory. And there was no crossing the street now.

The Judgment of Eternity and the Burden of Sin

Behind the difficulty of recognizing sins and repenting of them stands the judgment of eternity, firm, true, and fair. When human actions are right, when believers see their own sins for what they are and repent of them, they feel they have brought their own judgments into alignment with a higher, truer standard. But one way or another, the judgment of eternity casts an indirect light on every human deed, endowing it with special weight. And whether people acknowledge their sins or not, sin retains this stubborn objectivity, its reality in the eyes of God. Believers are aware of the judgment of eternity looming behind them; on some level they may also have some inkling of how they stand.

This special objectivity, the weight of sin, is what makes it such a burden. Sins are the heaviest burdens people carry and the greatest impediments to a simple life. They weigh us down and threaten to sink the fragile vessel of a human life. Sin also ties both victim and perpetrator to the past, preventing genuine forward movement. Every future event becomes instead a replay of old scenes.

If simplicity of life is a moving virtue, it must consist in an ongoing act of unburdening oneself. When Christians acknowledge their sins and repent of them, they jettison their heaviest cargo and slip the cable that ties them to the past. Their lives are able to move forward at a steady pace only, in fact, if they have acquired the habit of regularly acknowledging their sins. As life moves forward, the future also becomes genuinely new.

It is no accident that the forgiveness of sins is so central to the Gospel and to the life of the church, no accident that Christ instituted a sacrament for the forgiveness of sins. The sacrament addresses the central human plight of sin, of knowing and repenting of our sins, and offers the gift of forgiveness. If Jesus means freedom, that freedom is first experienced in the forgiveness of sins and the consequent disencumbering of human life. The practice of simplicity of life consists in the ability to keep life moving by discarding the burden of sin, a tandem act of grace and nature, of God's grace and human courage. Christians are also reminded that forgiveness is not a tit-for-tat exchange but always *first* a giving, quite apart from the response they receive. Likewise, when they themselves are forgiven, they are the recipients of a gift they have not earned.

If, like genetic coding, God's Providence writes in fine print, it should be no surprise that God's grace does not first act in great events, announcing its presence in a thunderclap. Rather grace flows quietly through the smallest interstices that lead from one human act to another. The knowledge that simplicity of life brings, like all forms of connatural knowledge, does not broaden Christians the way learning a new skill does. Instead, this knowledge deepens in them, as God's will enters ever more fully into their lives. It is the presence of Christ that simplifies human life. We must hollow out a circle in our lives and wait for his presence to fill it. Ultimately, Christians pray for a single gift: that Christ give us an undivided heart. *Jesus meek and humble of heart make our hearts like unto thine.*

Chapter Six

THE CHALLENGE OF CELIBACY

THE PRACTICE OF CELIBACY

I F THE CHALLENGE of simplicity of life is broad and open-ended, what holds human life together and gives it meaning, the challenge of celibacy is focused and specific, to forgo marriage and family and to live a chaste, celibate life as a witness to the power of God's kingdom, present and active in this world. In one sense the challenge remains constant from age to age; in another, it is shaped by the social milieu in which a celibate commitment is made and in which a celibate life is lived. This larger social setting is the first topic of consideration, since it frames any realistic look at the practice of celibacy.

Celibacy is always practiced against the background of society's understanding of marriage and sexuality. If marriage experiences difficulty, celibacy will too. It will no longer be intelligible. If society's understanding of long-term commitment is impaired, both will suffer. Dramatic changes have occurred on these fronts in recent decades.

Sexuality in American culture has been increasingly separated from marriage and children. Instead, it has grown into a largely pleasure-based, often morally neutral activity of a casual nature: sex demystified. No big deal. It is a natural urge, different but not far distant from other human appetites. The question is not *why* engage in sex, but *why not!* This message has been communicated to young and not so young people now for two generations. And from multiple sources: not just from movies and television, but from sex education manuals and, on occasion, from the surgeon general, and it has had a major impact on the way ordinary people act.

98

Yet centuries of tradition that say the opposite will not go easily or quietly into the night. There are also a growing number of teens who have chosen to practice abstinence, remarkable given the lack of encouragement for such behavior in this age group, which is subject both to raging hormones and strong peer pressure. It has also become clear that many adults, religious or not, have come to feel that human sexuality always has an emotional, indeed a spiritual dimension. Hence to have casual sex anytime with just about anyone is coarsening. It does bad things to good people. The phenomenon of "secondary virginity," has grown out of this mood, growing numbers of men and women who decide to practice abstinence for a time as a special preparation for marriage.[1]

The truth is that society may be having second thoughts about permissive attitudes toward sex. Or maybe not. But one thing is perfectly clear. Society right now sends out very mixed signals about sexuality. On the one hand, a message of encouragement. First, one meets the circle of natural sexuality about which the sex education manuals speak, accompanied by the wonderful admonition to teenagers, the epitome of mixed messages, "Be responsible, but carry a condom." The various liberation movements constitute a second circle. Here the message of sexual freedom has gone forth to gay, lesbian, bisexual, and transgendered men and women: their lifestyle and activity deserve toleration and respect. The circle of sexual freedom widens.

Yet these circles are surrounded on all sides by barbed wire fences of sexual misconduct laws, many of which carry very serious penalties and make sense, but some of which are quite subjective, able to be easily broken. Step one foot outside the circle in the wrong direction and a person can land in serious trouble — be suspended from school, jeopardize a job, or be sued.

What happens at the end of an orientation program in school or business these days? The concluding gesture is the distribution of a written sexual misconduct policy. New students or employees are then asked to sign on the dotted line that they have received the document, thereby reducing the institution's liability. This is necessary because no one is quite sure where the line is between the circles of sexual freedom that mean pleasure and the barbed wire fences that mean big trouble. And the gray areas are becoming ever grayer. The legal thicket of heterosexual male-on-male sexual harassment claims prompted a federal judge in Georgia to predict last year that plain and simple vulgar conduct "will soon doom enforcement of all sexual-harassment law and compel American workers simply to accept a certain amount of 'boorish behavior' on the job."[2] Yet as these issues percolate through the court system, it has become accepted that if a person of either sex drapes an arm around the shoulder of a secretary or co-worker too many times in school or at work, he or she could be in serious trouble. Curiously, the old taboos that have surrounded human sexuality seem ineluctably to have snuck in by the backdoor, to reappear in the guise of these most modern dilemmas.

This is the situation facing a young man when he makes a promise of celibacy: a society in which the social consensus, the middle ground about sexuality — *what may be taken for granted as custom* — has broken down, and people are caught between two fires: the circles of sexual freedom and the sexual harassment laws that surround them on every side.

Priestly celibacy will function in a special way in this cultural context. Two generations ago, a celibate commitment was widely respected because of the sacrifice of spouse and family it entailed. It still may involve such a sacrifice, but as a public gesture it is greeted today with puzzlement as an action largely devoid of positive meaning. Instead, a template of suspicion descends: the celibate as sexual suspect. What is he or she hiding or avoiding? It has also becomes less a matter of private conduct. In practice, priestly celibacy today is a public test case and a prime example of church teachings that fly against regnant cultural attitudes on sexuality, marriage, family, and the life issues. In other words, if practiced with integrity, priestly celibacy exemplifies the truth of other countercultural teachings. People say, "Although it may not make complete sense to us, this group practices what it preaches." They tell others to follow a strict standard and they hold to it first themselves. Priestly lifestyles seriously strengthen the general credibility of the church.

They can also seriously weaken it. Lapses in a priest's personal behavior call into question the countercultural values — regarding sexuality, family, the life issues — to which the church witnesses. And there is an audience quick to say. "See, they say one thing but do another themselves." Predictably, such lapses also have a trickle-down effect, giving the apparent lie to other church teachings. How seriously, for example, should the church's ban on the ordination of women be taken? Is this an apostolic tradition that cannot be changed or simply the defensive posture of a misogynist gerontocracy? In short, the *personal* lapses of priests and bishops undermine the *public* teaching of the church. For that reason, the general credibility of the church's public teaching authority rides on the integrity of a priest's practice of celibacy.

These factors were present before the sex scandals of 2002 began to unfold. Those revelations have not altered the fundamentals, but the scandals have radicalized the discussion, *reversing public presumptions* about the conduct of priests and bishops. This was a step of major importance that changed the terrain for priests and bishops in every way. It therefore bears closer examination. Why did the revelations from January to June 2002 make such an indelible impression? There were high profile pedophile priests before these scandals, Gilbert Gauthe of Lafayette, Louisiana, and James Porter of Fall River, Massachusetts. Perhaps the trio who lent faces to this phase of the scandal made the difference.

THE REVERSAL OF PRESUMPTIONS

Cardinal Bernard Law of Boston and former priests John J. Geoghan and Paul R. Shanley made a deep impression. As information emerged from Boston, it became clear that Cardinal Law knew more than he first admitted. Then, inch by inch, more information and apologies were extracted from the archdiocese. It was also clear that when decisions about abusive priests were made by other church officials, the cardinal was not quick to assume ultimate responsibility. Where did the buck stop? While old quarrels with the

Boston Globe *may have fueled investigative bloodlust, the press did not invent the story of serious negligence.*

But Cardinal Law was not just any bishop. He was the senior American cardinal, perhaps the most trusted American in Rome, arguably the most powerful Catholic prelate in the United States. If he was not trustworthy, then who was? After the scandals, the template of Cardinal Law slipped down over the portrait of every other bishop, and they were judged on the basis of his conduct. The public presumption on other bishops was reversed. Were they any different from Cardinal Law? The burden now lay on them to prove otherwise.

What Cardinal Law did for bishops, Shanley and Geoghan did for priests. Shanley began as an activist "street priest." He was a sexual abuser by conviction. One of his causes was the North American Man Boy Love Alliance (NAMBLA.) Here was one nightmare. John Geoghan was another. At his trial, he looked like the dependable Irish-American priest who never missed a communion call. But Geoghan's mild exterior camouflaged a sexual predator with a prodigious appetite for children. Geoghan and Shanley provided a template that slipped over the picture of other American priests. Would you now trust your teenagers with a priest? This was the question that priests now faced. The burden lay on them to prove otherwise.

Once lost, a reputation is regained only through a slow, arduous process. Only a new generation of priests and bishops who are conscientious about their duties and honest about celibate living can perform that task. A notable side effect of these scandals is to solder the discipline of celibacy to the priesthood for the foreseeable future. Celibacy has become an albatross that must be made into a virtue, with the fortunes of the priesthood rising or falling on its practice. Predictable consequences should follow. Dioceses and seminaries should be very cautious about accepting seminary candidates when there are sexual risk factors. Zero tolerance on sexual abuse will make the church as a whole more vigilant and more observant in every way on celibate living.

Because of the breakdown of social custom, of what may be assumed, and because of how much rides on the integrity of a celibate commitment, seminaries are now forced to talk more openly and frankly with candidates about sexuality and celibacy. It would be very odd if they did not. It would be as if one heard frank talk all around about sexuality, while the church sat mum or minced words, especially after so much damage on this score. So much talk is related to so much law. Both are symptoms of the breakdown of social custom, of what may currently be taken for granted about sexual behavior. Seminaries must now discuss what other ages and societies had assumed and could leave unspoken. They hope that a seminarian's own informed, voluntary choice, supported by a community of committed, like-minded people, will help him live a celibate commitment with integrity. Therefore the challenge of celibacy today is to move from a discipline enforced by social taboo in past generations to a commitment consciously, deliberately, freely made in the context of a supportive community of conscientious priests and laity.

Hence the seminary must talk very frankly about sexuality and how it bears on a celibate commitment. In deliberately addressing the topic, the groundwork is set for the strong, deliberate choice of a celibate life by seminarians. This course is not simple or without its own dangers. To make so much ride on individual decision is to place a heavy burden on young shoulders For this reason the social consensus among seminarians and priests on celibate living has never been more important. What constitutes an honest and integral celibate commitment? How much will the social group tolerate in regard to peer misconduct? Surely it is a special responsibility of seminary officials and bishops to enforce the rules on celibate living, but every priest and seminarian is co-responsible as well. The priesthood is a corporate charism and a worldwide *ordo* and the group precedes the inclusion of any individual into it. From many points of view, it should be evident that an individual priest's reputation rises or falls on the behavior of others.

If the topic of sexuality is to be addressed in a more direct and forthright way, the first subject of consideration is sexual orientation. That the topic is now treated openly would have shocked

many in earlier generations, because it constitutes a public statement that there are homosexual seminarians, priests, and bishops,
and they face very different challenges in regard to celibate living.
Of course, that fact was known but never publicly acknowledged.

However, the social climate has changed dramatically. To refrain
from talking about sexual orientation now would be a very strange
posture in our society and surely one that lets fear take the upper
hand. For while some scruple to talk about sexual orientation, children who watch daytime television are treated to a steady diet of
high-profile sexual behavior, the more eye-catching the better: bi-
sexuals who cannot make up their mind; transgendered couples
now having second thoughts, etc. Everyone talks about everything
and no one blinks. If seminaries fail to talk about sexual orientation, they have ceded the field of effective control to the public
media or to the arena of backdoor gossip. The topic deserves a better fate than that, and too much rides on its outcome to remain
silent.

The obvious should then be acknowledged. Heterosexual seminarians face a distinctive challenge. They easily blend into the
culture from which they came. Young men who leave the seminary
quickly take up the dating habits of their contemporaries. They re-
vert to type. But in the seminary they often do not act out and
if they do so, they act alone and secretively, feeling guilty at the
end. The challenge for them is to open up to an advisor or spiritual
director and talk about the situation in their lives.

With homosexual seminarians and priests, the challenge is different. The role of the social group is paramount. This is the *novum*
in the modern phenomenon of homosexuality: the role of the gay
community. While the social glue that holds priests together in a
presbyterate has grown weaker, the sense of belonging in the gay
community has become stronger. This poses its own challenge for
homosexual priests and seminarians. To which community does
one owe first allegiance, the priesthood or the gay community?
The general question quickly becomes more particular. How tolerant of misconduct or how observant of the rules are homosexual
priests and seminarians among themselves? If they are tolerant of

misconduct, how independent will individual priests or seminarians be from a group that promotes a lifestyle contrary to a celibate commitment?

There may be tensions among people on these issues in a seminary community or in a presbyterate. There are everywhere else that such matters arise. Sexual orientation is a very deeply felt, private part of a person. Differences here are often very threatening. One can count on the fact that there is nothing more puzzling than another person's sexual struggles if they are a millimeter different from one's own. This is a valuable lesson in its own right.

While the challenge of celibacy may be different, the social rules on celibate living, the rules of conduct, must be the same for everyone in the seminary and in the priesthood. Celibacy is socially defined by the church and not open to private interpretation. It means at minimum — the social bottom line — that a seminarian or a priest is not having sex with another person on a regular or even occasional basis. The "developmental" approach that regarded lapses as small missteps in a larger growth trajectory has long been abandoned. If a seminarian lapses, he should leave of his own volition or be invited to leave. Experience has taught us that lapses, like grapes, grow in bunches. This is where zero tolerance makes sense and should begin.

Experience has also taught us that if the *bottom line* is not in place, then the *higher motivation* will never be taken seriously. Instead, elevated language will be regarded as a sop for the naive as the worldly-wise smile to themselves. And the bottom line must be the same for everyone, although the challenge facing men in a community or in a presbyterate will be different.

But simply to speak of the bottom line does not suffice. The rabbis spoke about a fence around the law. The Catholic tradition speaks of sin and the near occasion of sin. In other words, there are signposts around an integral celebrate commitment that tell a seminarian or a priest that his actions are leading in the right or wrong direction, and these should be heeded. An integral celibate commitment, for example, includes the nature of one's relationships with others. It is a wonderful thing for a celibate man to have many friends, both men and women, but it is not a wonderful thing when friendship becomes romance. Celibacy also includes what one reads, watches on television, and sees in movies. The places one frequents, bars or locales where sex is the commodity of trade, are a concern. Dangers hit with special force in regard to the Internet, with availability, apparent anonymity, and the addictive nature of Internet pornography. These are part of a slippery slope in the wrong direction.

Fortunately, if a seminarian's life is filled with good friendships and his mind with good reading, if he seeks the advice of those more experienced when he is confused, then he has taken steps in the right direction.

When the practice is in place, then the value of celibacy can be seriously considered. The church calls the present generation of priests and seminarians to embrace the value of celibacy in a conscious and deliberate way and so to live their lives in accord with its vision, and this is the topic to which we now turn.

THE VALUE OF CELIBACY

Celibacy in the Family

Celibacy is an ancient religious practice found in religions and cultures in both East and West. It is rooted in the family and in that element of restraint that elevates human sexuality above its animal origins. In this regard, it is important to recall that the words "father," "mother," "sister," and "brother" are, strictly speaking, human terms with no exact equivalents in the animal world. While animals occasionally bond for life, most wander off after mating with little sense of lingering kinship. By contrast, the human family represents a cultural achievement of our earliest ancestors, the first pitons placed in the sheer granite wall humans had to scale to distinguish themselves from their instinctual origins. It is equally an achievement that must be renewed in every generation.

The words "father," "mother," "sister," and "brother" remind us of the element of conscious restraint that prevents a father from having sex with his daughter or a mother with her son or a brother with his sister. This restraint forms the curvature of the family circle, making the human family into a zone of peace in which children can be raised with dignity and respect. Human sexuality in its own right also represents a cultural achievement in which the force of sexual drive and instinct are balanced by those of affection and restraint. When the elements of affection and restraint are totally missing, when humans rut like animals, it seems not only wrong but unnatural in its own way. Celibacy is built into both the protective curvature of the family circle and of human sexuality. Celibacy is born in the center of the family. This restraint is also balanced by something more positive, a broad, gentle love of a father for his daughter or a sister for her brother.

Celibacy in the Scriptures

Jesus's preaching of the kingdom of God abounds in images of the family. Jesus prays to God as *Abba*, Father, and teaches his disciples to do the same. The great prayer that Jesus bequeaths to his followers begins in the Gospel of Luke with the simple word "Father." The disciples are told to regard God as Jesus did and so to pray to him as "Father" and see themselves as his children. The "child" thus became the first image of the disciple. In the third chapter of Mark's Gospel, it is clear that Jesus's own first family are not his natural kin but those who hear the word of God and keep it. They are truly mother and brother and sister to him. In this way, Jesus exponentially expands the human family. In light of the coming of God's kingdom, even the stranger and alien, if they hear the word of God and keep it, can become brothers and sisters, members of the family of faith. The human family as a zone of peace expands into that peaceable kingdom in which all creation gathers in harmony and accord around the banquet table of God, the father. Jesus's natural family, although superseded, are not rejected but uniquely included in the family of faith. In Luke, they are counted among his followers. Indeed, Luke tells us that Jesus is conceived in the Virgin's womb through her response to the Angel's word. In effect, she hears the Word of God and keeps it, the mark of a disciple.

Jesus's own celibacy is a symbolic gesture that fittingly embodies his commitment. His intimacy with God and his preaching of the kingdom are all-consuming. As Jesus transcends the limits of a single family, he does so to give himself ever more fully to his Father in heaven and his family of believers on earth, and there is no departure from this single-minded dedication. Jesus also raises the possibility of celibacy for some disciples "for the sake of the kingdom of heaven" (Matt. 19:10–12). Like marriage without divorce, celibacy is an eschatological virtue that exceeds what the world deems possible.[3] He regards it as a special gift. When St. Paul turns to the topic (1 Cor. 7:7–9, 25–38), it is likewise in the context of the age to come. Paul expects the imminent end of this age and gives his followers practical advice. He wants everyone to remain in their present state because time is short and the parousia near.[4] Both of these passages place celibacy in the context of the kingdom and the eschatological accent has remained central in Christian tradition. They also provide a basis for reflection on enduring moral guidance. Reflecting on the Gospel in light of its experience, Christian tradition becomes the author of celibacy as a way of life for ordained ministers.

Celibacy in the Church

Over the centuries, the church has witnessed to the truths of the Gospel in diverse ways. At the beginning of the second millennium as part of the reforms of Pope Gregory VII (1073–85), the church wove the discipline of celibacy into a way of life for diocesan clergy, and this is where it finds its proper meaning.

Celibacy is only one part of a priestly way of life and belongs in a larger context to make sense. The debate about optional vs. mandatory celibacy has had an unfortunate way of isolating the topic. If the current scandals return it to center stage isolation, that will continue to shed a false light on the discipline. Rather, celibacy follows from prayer and belongs with simplicity of life and obedience.

Celibacy is part of the special logic of priestly life, as the roles of husband and wife are part of the logic of marriage. This context also supplies a dynamic element that is clearly expressed in the ceremony of ordination to the diaconate and priesthood. Here the church brings together the terms of contract to which a young man agrees as his subjective contribution to the objective reception of the sacrament. At the reception of the sacrament, he publicly pledges to recite the Liturgy of the Hours. He pledges to be a man of prayer who daily prays for the church. This sets the stage for the promises of celibacy and obedience. A priest gives up marriage and family. Instead he promises to bestow on the people he serves the love, affection, and devotion he would have given to a natural family. He is called "father" and regards those he serves as "brothers" and "sisters." As he gives up one kind of family, he gains another, a family of faith.

His promise of obedience is akin to a marriage vow. The promise is made to the office of bishop, but the ultimate recipients are Almighty God and the people he serves. He promises to be present in good and bad times, until death ends the contract. In order to make good on this pledge, he places the determination of pastoral need in the hands of the bishop, whose ministry is to the whole local church. Consciously, he pledges his willingness to have his life turned upside down from time to time in order to better serve the family of faith to whom he is pledged. Often, it turns out to be good for him as well. Just as parents are forced to grow in unexpected ways by the insistent but not always reasonable demands of family, so too priests grow as they seek to meet the unexpected needs of their parishioners.

This complex transaction takes place in the context of a sacrament. This underscores that a priestly way of life exceeds the natural powers of any individual. Rather, it is a witness to the power of God's kingdom, guiding the church and forming the lives of Christians. Celibacy in the context of priestly life is lived in the power of God's kingdom present and active in an individual life. Therefore it is a mistake to try to interpret or justify celibacy in functional terms, e.g., because a priest is unmarried, he can devote more time to his flock than his married Protestant counterpart. De facto, this is often not the case. It also misunderstands the issue. Celibacy in the context of priestly life is first a symbolic, religious gesture, a special witness to the power of God's kingdom and to Christ's special presence in the life of one person.

In the ceremony of ordination, an ideal is proposed to a young man as the sacrament of Orders is bestowed. Priests may not live up to this ideal. The ideal itself may not be currently in vogue, but it is strong and, in the Roman rite, it has stood the test of a millennium. It will not go easily or quietly into the night.

Chapter Seven

THE CHALLENGE OF AUTHORITY AND OBEDIENCE

THE CHALLENGE OF AUTHORITY

AUTHORITY AND OBEDIENCE are correlate terms that take on special meaning in a religious context. Religious obedience is rendered to those who legitimately claim moral or spiritual authority. This is not the same as following directions from someone higher on the organizational flow chart or taking orders from the boss at work. Still, religious authority is exercised and interpreted against the background of our society. The comparison drawn about celibacy also applies here. Just as celibacy is understood against the background of society's assumptions about marriage and sexuality, so religious authority is exercised against the backdrop of society's understanding of authority in general and moral authority in particular.

The Modern Dilemma

However, authority in just such terms has come upon hard times, and this situation will frame how church authority is interpreted and religious obedience is given in today's world.

The story is long, and only its critical stages are highlighted here. The modern era began in the seventeenth century in the wake of the Thirty Years War (1618–48) when the authority of religious tradition was superseded by that of autonomous reason. The reign of autonomous reason was relatively brief. In the nineteenth century, Arthur Schopenhauer and Friedrich Nietzsche argued eloquently and forcefully that will, not reason, was the major factor. For Karl Marx, what society termed "rational" at any time only served to cloak the dominant interests of its leading socioeconomic class.

111

Sigmund Freud took the argument inside. Conscious reason was only the surface instrument of hidden, unconscious factors, the real determinants of behavior. For Max Weber, instrumental reason finally fashioned an iron cage of efficiency, devoid of larger purpose, in which humanity was trapped.

But the central discussion of authority in the past century was not framed by thinkers at all. Following World War I, two great quasi-religious ideologies made successive claims to moral authority. Nazism and Communism were secular engines of salvation that sought to translate religious promises into earthly realities, original sin into programs of racial purity or social improvement, steps on the road to an earthly heaven: a thousand-year Reich or a classless utopia. Both these twentieth-century ideologies of salvation have collapsed. In retrospect, they can only be regarded as terrible human mistakes without redeeming value. The Communist experiment enjoyed the doubtful cáchet of a world empire, albeit of brief duration, that bequeathed no monuments to posterity. On the contrary, Eastern Europe after 1989 resembled little more than a junkyard, abandoned by careless owners bent on a hasty departure. Still, the moral tensions of the Cold War, which divided the world into political camps, each claiming legitimate authority, Free West vs. Communist East, held many other values in place. With the fall of the Berlin Wall in 1989, this entire house of cards collapsed.

The Vacuum of Authority

This preamble serves to underscore a single conclusion: there is a widespread vacuum of authority in Western society. Fooled more than once, modern consciousness can only trust its suspicious instincts. The current vogue of thinkers like Derrida and Foucault is both ironic and instructive; here suspicion itself becomes an authority.

The vacuum of authority takes on a special character in the United States. From the start, the United States regarded itself as country endowed with moral purpose. This self-understanding was put to a stern test by the Vietnam War and the near impeachment of a president in 1973. Traditional institutions were dealt deeply discrediting blows. The era has spawned a complex legacy. Movements of emancipation organized on the basis of race, gender, and sexuality continue to claim moral high ground. Suspicion of institutions continues unabated. Traditional constraints on the behavior of individuals and groups have steadily eroded. The social fabric wears thin. The only commonly accepted values across the spectrum are *procedural* ones: tolerance and choice.

One step beyond procedure, society breaks into sharply opposed camps, into culture wars. A prime example is abortion. Religious and political conservatives stand staunchly opposed; liberal opinion stands in favor. No middle ground seems to exist. Hence, in our polarized society, on *substantive* issues the court system has become the arena of first, not last, resort. Court dockets are clogged with contentious social conflicts — over civil rights, abortion, sexual discrimination — that custom can no longer mediate. What was said in regard to sexuality can be repeated here. So many cases before the courts and so much talk in the media are symptoms of a society in which custom — what may be taken for granted — plays a smaller and smaller role.

The result is a highly litigious, atomized society. Contentious social and moral issues that the court cannot mediate are regularly referred to the individual for decision. In some quarters, "choice" is the preferred solution. But in a sea of social permissiveness, individuals and families often stagger under the weight of moral decision-making now thrust on their shoulders.

Clearly as well, this broad-based skepticism is not first a creature of theory. On the contrary, it has spawned a social atmosphere that daily greets the average citizen. Grade school children are fully capable of warning teachers about an eighth grader's legal rights. Parents regularly berate teachers and school boards for neglecting the education of their children. They invariably side with their children when the latter are caught cheating red-handed. Irate parents have been known to assault the local soccer coach when they disagree with him. In the meantime, parents are fortunate to retain effective control over teenage children.

Our is also the age of the "second opinion" in medical matters. Doctors are burdened by the cost of malpractice insurance, so quick are patients to sue. In a suspicious, litigious society, the only ones who profit are lawyers. The plain fact is that legitimate authority stands everywhere under a cloud of suspicion. All around are the fallen icons of former eras: the FBI, the CIA, the State of Israel, the House of Windsor, Enron, Arthur Andersen, the *New York Times*, the Catholic Church.

The present vacuum of authority is curious for another reason. For while it produces suspicion on the one hand, it creates a climate of superstition on the other, simultaneously a rejection of authority and a yearning for it. It is closer to the truth to describe this vague, undefined feeling as a longing for "something," more accurately, a feeling that "something is missing." The connection between the dilemma of authority and the search for spirituality is evident enough. Significantly, in most bookstores the section on self-help literature is far more extensive than the one on Western Civilization. The single individual, surrounded by suspect institutions, is left to his or her own devices. The great virtue of the age, "choice," quickly becomes a burden, and so people look for answers where ever they can find them. Dr. Phil solves problems in the audience and over the phone and people can't wait to call. Crystals, massage therapy, and Eastern religions provide answers for some, or at least reduce tension. A creation-based spirituality center in northern California maintained a resident witch, a representative of the Wicca religion, so wide is the net thrown. Certainly as well, in this skeptical age in which God, Christ, Trinity, and the Catholic Church often find themselves in serious trouble, the belief in angels flourishes just about everywhere.

The Church's Authority

In such a society, the church's authority strikes sparks in all directions. On the one hand, it appears highly attractive. On the other, it is difficult to understand and open to serious misunderstanding. Certainly the church will be forced to struggle to make its claim to authority clear in its own terms.

First, the attraction. In the present vacuum, the church's claim to teach with authority speaks to the enormous hunger of people to find a safe haven as they struggle with the burden of so much personal choice. These days people literally plead for help. As more responsibility is thrust on individuals and families, they become increasingly aware of their own inability to make sense out of the world in which they live.

This has been a true source of the church's attraction, which the vacuum of authority in the modern world highlights. The church offers answers. But the hungers of the modern world may outrun what the Catholic Church has to offer. Religious fundamentalism grows throughout the world because of the way it cuts through complex problems to offer simple answers. Catholicism can only go so far down this road. G. K. Chesterton summed up the Catholic view. Human life comprises a complex problem that calls for a complex answer.[1]

Hence, it is not possible, past a point, to cut Catholic doctrine down to simple size. For the same reason, religious fundamentalism probably does not find a good home in the Catholic tradition and certainly not in a classic Catholic consciousness. On the contrary, representative Catholic types over the ages — Thomas Aquinas, Thomas More, Blaise Pascal, John Henry Newman, G. K. Chesterton — display a complex, differentiated mind-set, the product of centuries of legal and philosophical disputation, akin to that of scholars of the Talmud. Here in a nutshell is also the Catholic objection to fundamentalism: the desire for authority pure and simple outstrips the patience required to make sure the authority is a *true* one. The strong desire for certitude also means that people will follow the doctrines that speak to their hungers. The latter seldom comprise a balanced diet.

The church's authority is misunderstood in another way. Because the church has steadfastly maintained unpopular positions on controversial issues, the impression exists that the Catholic Church is a highly authoritarian institution. But this is really not the case. The traditional teaching about "theological notes" is instructive here. In the neoscholastic tradition, each doctrine was assigned a "note" or doctrinal classification on a sliding scale from defined truth to common opinion.

This approach is indicative of a church that carefully weighs the degree of authority it wishes to engage as it proposes various truths for belief. The doctrine of theological notes is an objective reflection of the differentiated consciousness described above. The same effort continues in the careful use of titles or superscripts in church documents. Most people pass over them without a second thought, but that is a mistake. The title is a shorthand description of the authoritative weight of the document. The distinctions in the documents of Vatican II — "constitutions," "decrees," and "declarations" — are significant. The church as a teacher may be fairly compared to a golfer with five woods, nine irons, and a sand wedge. It selects various clubs to engage different degrees of authority. That authority is employed with such differentiation would come as a surprise not only to the general public but also to many Catholics.

Church teaching stands under a double imperative, the ends of which are not easy to hold together, much less reconcile. The supernatural imperative says the church's teaching comes from above. It is revelation. People may not be able to understand it fully themselves or explain it well to others; some doctrines may not speak at all in a particular age, e.g., the doctrine of original sin in the Enlightenment. Yet Catholics are bound to hold them. The natural imperative on the other hand says that the church must play by the same rules as everyone else in society. In the last analysis, it must persuade, and its authority is measured by the persuasiveness of its teaching.

The Credibility of the Church

The classic arguments that the church makes for its own authority are not first theoretical. Rather, the marks of the church — one, holy, catholic, and apostolic — are the source of its credibility. When these are on full display, the church and its teachings are believable. While the marks of the church are interrelated, each has a life of its own. Two speak clearly in the present age and are a special source of the church's authority: apostolicity and holiness.

First, apostolicity. The church has lasted. Pope John Paul II is reckoned the 261st successor of St. Peter, the oldest continuous office in an ancient religious tradition that has seen the rise and fall of the Roman Empire, the Byzantine Empire, the Holy Roman Empire, the monarchies of Europe, and Nazism and Communism.[2] It has outlasted them and it will outlast the problems of this age as well. The stability of the church in a changing, uncertain world is a strong argument in its favor and remains so today.

But the church has not endured by dint of inertial force, the way an old rock sits immobile and lifeless in a stream. It has lasted because of the continuing light the tradition sheds on the human predicament and because of the fruitfulness of the way of life it has called people to live over the ages. The capacity for distinction and differentiation has been a key to its longevity, allowing the tradition to remain firm yet flexible, like a strong bridge spanning distant shores, whose strength and stability lie in its ability to sway. Distinction and differentiation — sway — make for flexibility in adapting an old tradition to a new age while remaining in essence the same. A brittle tradition, on the other hand, would have collapsed centuries ago. And a fully fixed, immobile tradition is a dead one, a bridge over which human feet no longer cross.

The second note is holiness. A great argument for the church's credibility has been its ability to produce in our time, for example, a person of the magnitude of Mother Teresa of Calcutta. In a skeptical and doubting age, she was by any reckoning a saint, and there is no better witness to the church's authority. In this regard, John Paul II has sought to canonize saints in every country he has visited. In doing so, he underscores that while documents and canon law are important, the truth of the Catholic faith rests in the final analysis on its ability to transform lives and, on occasion, to produce women and men of extraordinary holiness. "The saint is the apology for the Christian revelation,"[3] writes Hans Urs von Balthasar. The saint is also the measure of the church's authority and the reason the church has lasted. One way or another, in a skeptical and suspicious age, the only argument that speaks convincingly is the force of personal witness.

For the same reason, the recent sexual abuse scandals have harmed the authority of the church. The force of bad witness has had its effect. It is difficult to assess the extent of the damage. Perhaps over time the witness of the great majority of priests, untainted by scandal, will emerge more forcefully. What is true in the midst of a difficult and confusing situation is that a special locus of the church's authority is the pastor of the local parish. If people still come to church in good numbers, surely a factor in this equation is the credible witness of the priests who serve them. The authority of the church in troubled waters rides on their shoulders in a special way. If their witness remains strong, then the church's authority holds firm at critical points, e.g., preaching, RCIA, catechesis.

HUMAN WEAKNESS IN JESUS'S FOLLOWERS

The church was founded on weak men. Peter, the prince of the apostles, denied Christ three times, a fact recorded in all the Gospels. Indeed, the Gospels are unanimous about the faults of Jesus's closest followers.

The tradition continued in the church and the failure of the clergy is an old story. Clerics do not appear in Dante's Inferno *in a flattering light. The weaknesses of the Renaissance popes are a matter of record: Alexander VI and his large family, Julius II, more general than religious leader. In Erasmus's satire, St. Peter himself comes forward to bar the gates of heaven against the final assault of this fiery warrior-pope. A story attributed to Napoleon sums up the matter. The emperor is once said to have remarked to his entourage that he intended to destroy the Catholic Church. "Good Luck, Sire," responded a courtier, doubtless a cleric, "the clergy have been trying to do it for centuries without great success."*

None of this excuses the failures of the clergy. But if the church were to have foundered on these grounds, it would have happened long ago. Indeed, if the Gospels are to be trusted, it would have died in Jerusalem. According to the Gospels, human weakness is the privileged place where God's grace shines through most brightly. But the shadow tradition remains in which human weakness simply begets its own kind, more sin and venality. The church has struggled with this dark shadow since its origins and continues to struggle with it at the beginning of the third millennium.

Authority in Seminary Formation

Because young men are trained not just as priests but as pastors these days, the proper exercise of authority becomes a special virtue toward which seminarians should aspire. That authority is exercised collaboratively adds an additional and significant nuance.

However, the seminary's approach to authority may seem indirect and remote from actual practice. In large measure, this has to do with the nature of priestly authority. The seminary takes as its starting point what the Gospel of Mark says about Jesus in chapter 1. The evangelist relates that Jesus taught with authority (Mark 1:22), and he says this before Jesus taught anything at all. It was the way he acted. If the scene were translated into simple human terms, it would be fair to say that Jesus acted as a man of *character.* This is the seminary's touchstone.

Character, Ralph Waldo Emerson wrote, has a "latent" quality that is essential to its nature, "a reserved force which acts directly by presence and without means." Why is it, he writes, that when some individuals appear, their "arrival alters the face of affairs?"[4] This kind of person examines arguments that others have reviewed endlessly without coming to a conclusion. But when he points to an answer, all heads nod. This is so because he speaks with authority.

For the proper exercise of authority in the future, seminary formation takes as a goal in the present the development of character, the ideal that Jesus sets in Mark's Gospel. How is character taught or communicated? Once again, the answer is indirect but clear enough from the way seminary formation is structured. Clerical education is a long, layered affair, philosophy then theology, introductory courses then more specialized study. While there is a pastoral component, the education essentially is not practical. If anything, the church has shown an aversion to hands-on training for priests in the belief that an immersion in the current vogue of practical answers is usually a one-way ticket to obsolescence.

The clear aim of seminary education is depth. This is not an immediately functional item. Instead, it builds up a large reservoir of knowledge, out of which flexible answers to unknown future problems might arise. This contributes to that latent quality of character of which Emerson speaks, the unspoken authority of one who possesses considerable reserves, who has many more cards in his hand that the ones he currently displays. "Half his strength he put not forth."[5] The combination of a long education with serious efforts to grow in prayer and the spiritual life provides a natural seedbed in which strength of character can grow. This is the goal of seminary formation.

If the force of personal witness is the credible voice that speaks to the age, the emphasis on character is calculated to develop and enhance its powers. Moreover, if the role of the priest today is so revealing of one's personal life, then, like it or not, a priest's character is relentlessly on display. Indeed, there is hardly an effective way in pastoral ministry to hide the taproots of personality or motivation. Seminary formation should face these facts squarely and strive to form men of character whose own personal witness can reliably inform the priestly role.

There are really few opportunities in seminary formation to exercise the kind of authority that comes to a man with ordination to the priesthood. Priestly authority is itself so symbolic, so rooted in the sacrament of Orders and so little functional that there is little opportunity for practice before hand. Seminarians, for example, are almost universally well-liked. Attired as priests, they are especially appealing, like puppies dressed for a special occasion. Yet even the most serious seminarian carries an innocuous air, connected in part to the absence of authority. This situation changes suddenly and dramatically at ordination. Only then does the full symbolic weight of the priesthood descend, endowing a man with the particular authority of the priestly role. No one is quite prepared for it. On the contrary, the first exercises of authority in the new role invariably bring large surprises to the new priest, revealing unknown layers of personality and hidden strengths and weaknesses. In this regard, the mistakes of newly ordained priests are common and predictable. To return to the golfing analogy, they often resemble golfers with only two clubs in their bag, a driver and a putter. They are either heavy-handed in their use of authority or they abdicate, avoiding its exercise. Only with time do priests learn to use the full range of clubs at their disposal. In other words, the *moderate* exercise of authority usually comes only after considerable practice.

In light of these considerations, seminary formation should focus on long-range goals. The priesthood involves a lifetime commitment and priestly formation should focus on qualities that help a man fulfill such a commitment worthily and fruitfully. Seminary years often make a deep impact and a lasting impression. Character traits, absorbed in formation, are often grafted directly on to a man's personality. Therefore, attitudes and viewpoints acquired in the seminary have a unique way of sticking. Though priests continue to grow throughout life, parts of their personality are set for life at ordination. This may be a cause for chagrin or rejoicing, but it is a stubborn fact.

The traditional comparison between seminary years and the hidden life of Christ is worth pondering. Jesus lived a hidden life of thirty years; then he appeared out of nowhere to begin teaching with authority, as the Gospel of Mark describes. Likewise, seminary years are a time of preparation, of relative seclusion, a time for study, for personal and spiritual growth. When a man is ordained he is expected to act with the full authority of the priestly office, and while that expectation may take some getting used to, it begins in earnest at ordination.

THE CHALLENGE OF OBEDIENCE

The Promise of Obedience

While seminary years may offer little opportunity to exercise priestly authority, the opposite seems true of obedience. The seminary offers ample practice in this virtue. Still, a formal promise of obedience is only made in the final years of formation, at ordination to the diaconate and priesthood, when the bond between priest and bishop is formally sealed. The ordination ceremony is the best place to begin to understand the nature of priestly obedience.

Next to the laying on of hands — the actual sacramental conferral of the priesthood — the promise of obedience is perhaps the most dramatic part of the ordination ceremony. The hands of the candidate for ordination are placed in those of the bishop. The gesture says it all: the surrender of control over one's own destiny. The accompanying words expand the gesture. The bishop asks the ordinand to make a twofold promise: first, "respect and obedience," then "to me and my successors." It is hard to imagine a more fateful commitment. An ordained priest will live through the term of five or six bishops. Some he will like; others he will not. Some he will gladly obey; others he will obey but not respect. This promise of obedience covers all future contingencies. The Council of Trent warns that the sacrament of Orders should not be conferred on children, nor, one may infer, the promise of obedience asked of a boy.

Like all such promises, the promise of obedience is made to God through the office of the bishop, but it is also a promise of service to the people of a diocese. It represents an enormous personal and public commitment with consequences far beyond the foreseeable future. If the law of unforeseen consequences roams free at an ordination to the priesthood, its favorite haunt is the promise of obedience.

The promise has been open to differing yet legitimate interpretations over the years. In the modern church, St. Ignatius and the Jesuits have had a special relationship to the virtue of obedience. In asking obedience of a priest, the superior seeks to discern the movement of the Spirit in his life in light of the Society's mission. (The wider lesson is that if one asks much of an individual by way of obedience, such demands are credible and effective only when they are matched by a large sensitivity to the individual and to the movement of the Spirit in his life.)

Obedience among diocesan priests has sometimes slipped into more secular modes. In the church before Vatican II, the pastor of a large urban parish endowed with special status related to the bishop the way a count or a duke might relate to a king. In such circumstances, there was rarely a thought about the discernment of the spirit. Instead a certain wary caution and prudent respect governed the way such independent players related to one another.

Today challenges to the promise of obedience may come from another side. While personnel boards perform an admirable service brokering positions among priests, they are not the recipients of a promise of obedience. Likewise, while organizational efficiency, personal satisfaction, and mutual convenience are values, obedience is a religious commitment, made to a bishop, regularly involving inconvenience and sacrifice. Vatican II lists humility and obedience first among the special spiritual requirements in the life of a priest.[6]

In doing so, the council sets the accent for the future, firmly establishing the promise of obedience for diocesan priests in a spiritual context.

The Religious Significance of Obedience

It is especially important to understand the religious significance of obedience. The great model is Jesus himself. His words in the garden before his death are human and direct. "Father, if you are willing, remove this cup from me; yet, not my will but yours be done" (Luke 22:42). Jesus dies on behalf of sinners in obedience to the Father's will. The Gospels make the connection to his followers explicit. Mark establishes the clear parallel between Jesus's self-understanding and the role of a disciple and his conclusion rings down the ages. "If any want to become my followers, let them deny themselves and take up their cross and follow me" (Mark 8:34).

The weakness of Jesus's closest followers during his actual ministry inextricably combines historical truth and theological interpretation and belongs to the primitive strata of the Gospel. No one would have concocted such stories. No one would have imagined their outcome. During Jesus's earthly ministry, the disciples repeatedly misunderstood his teaching. Mark entwines Jesus's threefold prediction of his passion with his disciples' venal misunderstanding. At the passion, misunderstanding springs into action. His closest followers betray, deny, and abandon him. Jesus dies alone. Clearly the appearances of the risen Jesus bestow a special gift. Jesus does not first appear to neutral bystanders but to the very disciples who denied and abandoned him. His first act is to forgive their betrayal, and this forgiveness becomes for them a moment of personal transformation. The Spirit who raised Jesus from the dead now changes his followers from weak, fearful men into forceful preachers, able now to carry the message of Jesus into the world. Their witness is always twofold. They testify that God's Spirit raised Jesus from the dead, and that the same Spirit changed and transformed their lives, bringing them from sin and death to new life in Christ.

The message of Jesus has always been carried on the shoulders of weak followers, and this been both its genius and its Achilles' heel. What Chesterton wrote of Peter is true of the whole church. "All the empires and the kingdoms have failed, because of this inherent and continual weakness, that they were founded by strong men and upon strong men. But this one thing, the historic Christian church, was founded on a weak man, and for that reason it is indestructible. For no chain is stronger than its weakest link."[7] Human weakness starkly underscores that God's Spirit carries the church. Though God uses the natural gifts and talents of his followers, human weakness offers a privileged moment for God's grace to shine through. But the shadow tradition has also continued: in its best moments, it has made the church honest and humble about weakness in its members; in its worst, Judas continues to recruit followers and the church has been plagued by betrayal from within, its worst wounds self-inflicted.

The church has few illusions about the weaknesses of officeholders, of popes, bishops, and priests. Indeed, the promise of obedience by a priest to his bishop is made from one weak human vessel to another. The church has also had few illusions about the weaknesses of those who obey. Because of this, the essence of obedience is a form of prayerful listening. It seeks to discern God's voice in the cacophony of all too human voices. A priest listens for God's plan in his life in the mixed motives of bishops who speak and in the equally mixed motivations of priests who obey. There is always a reason to be cynical about authority, about the decisions of bishops who seek to fill holes and sometimes ask priests to take on tasks beyond them. But there are always stronger reasons to rise above such cynicism. Still, one must often struggle to maintain a religious sense of obedience when God's Providence in one's life is determined in critical instances by the decisions of a bishop, a weak, human vessel like oneself, to whom one has made a promise. For good or ill, this is the heart and mystery of the promise of obedience, the final stitch that knits prayer, simplicity, and celibacy into a single garment, a coherent way of life.

The Scandals and the Promise of Obedience

The sexual abuse scandals place a special strain on the promise of obedience, especially the promise that diocesan priests make to their bishop. While many factors lie in the realm of future imponderables, three stand out.

First, beginning in January 2002, the unrelenting media coverage of sexual misconduct by priests has created a climate in which almost all priests, certainly diocesan priests, could become the target of a charge of sexual misconduct in some form. It is easy to imagine an angry but clever parishioner or parish employee concocting a plausible but false allegation that is not easily discredited. Once such an allegation becomes public, perhaps in a lawsuit, a man's reputation is swiftly ruined. In the current climate, priests do not enjoy the presumption of innocence. For the foreseeable future, this sword of Damocles hangs over the head of all priests.

Second, bishops seem in much the same boat but in a different compartment. In order to reassure Catholics and other citizens, they embraced a policy of zero tolerance of sexual abuse of children and young people, an important and necessary action. But when that policy results in the removal of a priest from ministry on the basis of a single incident some thirty years ago, a question of fairness necessarily rises from another side. To compensate past victims must one create a few clerical victims in the present? Is this the unfortunate but unavoidable collateral damage the church must absorb to rectify a bad situation? The bishops occupy their own difficult position here. While some priests are punished *publicly,* bishops are punished *privately.* They know in their hearts they have not yet dealt publicly with the issue of episcopal complicity in priestly sexual misconduct. That sword of Damocles awaits them. But now they must devote great time and energy to sexual misconduct. They must show pastoral solicitude to victims, listen to legal and financial considerations, and, with the help of review boards, sort out true from false allegations.

Third, the relationship between priests and bishops is affected on all fronts. As legal, canonical, and financial considerations mount, they threaten to eclipse a bishop's pastoral solicitude toward his priests. As this solicitude diminishes, the religious dimension of the promise of obedience diminishes as well. The church seems to lessen its commitment to priests. Priests lessen their commitment to the church. The connecting tissue grows thin. What once was regarded as a lifelong vocation becomes instead a shaky job with few long-term guarantees. Just as Boeing and Kodak discharge unnecessary workers in a down economy, so the church with a sad and weary eye cuts its losses on future priestly liabilities. If bishops were accused of sheltering delinquent priests in the past, must they now demonstrate a new attitude by punishing clerical offenders, even old ones, with severity? This may not represent a fair estimate of a complex situation. But it is the impression in the mind of many priests.

THE IMPRESSION OF MANY PRIESTS

The bishop's secretary had telephoned. He got the message on his answering machine. Please return the call at your earliest convenience, a matter of some importance. So he called at once. The bishop wanted to see him the next afternoon. The secretary was noncommittal in a studied way.

The priest thought to himself, What could it be? He could think of only one thing. Someone had lodged an allegation of sexual misconduct. He wracked his brains. Who could it be and what might he have done? He came up with nothing. But he knew that did not necessarily matter. The next few hours he was on the phone to lawyers, canon lawyers and friends. What were his rights? What should his strategy be? Should he take a lawyer with him? The information he received was not consoling. He was told of a priest who had been temporarily removed, two years ago, because of an allegation received by phone on a sex abuse hotline. Two months ago, his friend Charlie was accused of impropriety on the basis of a "recovered" memory. A man visited a psychiatrist because of fear of flying, and therapy revealed the phobia was rooted in a childhood memory of "touching" by a priest. Charlie could barely remember the man. A suit and a claim were filed. The charge became public. That was enough for temporary removal.

The priest spent a sleepless night. He had a premonition that the meeting would spell the end of his life as a priest. The bishop was running late but received the priest cordially. He was clearly preoccupied. "I'm sorry to call you in at the last moment, but I have to meet with parishioners who have asked me to open a new parish on the east side. I don't need a firm answer, but would you be willing to consider it and can I say that to these people this evening? Can I mention your name? It would be encouraging news to them."

The priest was stunned. That was it? The bishop was asking him to start a new parish. The color drained from his face and then returned a bright red. "What's the matter?" the bishop asked.

"I thought I was going to be hit with an allegation of sexual misconduct."

"What?" said the bishop "You are one of my best priests."

"Look, Bishop, you say that to everyone who comes in here. You said that to Charlie two months ago."

"Well, he was — is — until that allegation came up. But believe me, I had no choice."

"Bishop, have you ever removed anyone because of these allegations that you returned to ministry?"

The bishop paused. "No . . . not yet, but I could and I certainly hope to do so in the future. But these things are very complicated." A long silence followed.

"Bishop, on second thought, I am not sure I want you to mention my name tonight. I need to think about my own options."

"Certainly, certainly," replied the bishop. "I only want to do what is best for you."

"Fine," the priest replied, "Sorry I can't help you."

When the priest left, the bishop slumped in his chair. It used to be a pleasure to be a bishop. But not any longer. The "fullness of the priesthood," he muttered to himself, was now often the pits.

PART THREE

THE OBJECTIVE GIFT

Chapter Eight

THE DOCTRINE OF
THE PRIESTHOOD

ornament

A s the Second Vatican Council recedes into the past, a clearer perspective is emerging about the scope and nature of its reforms for the church. One of those reforms, the renewal of the *priesthood in the presbyteral order,* is the focus of this chapter. This is the "degree" of the priesthood that belongs to ordinary diocesan or religious priests; by contrast, the bishop is now described as possessing the "fullness" of the priesthood. Such distinctions may be new to some readers.

DEVELOPMENT OF DOCTRINE

The best measure of any reform is the way in which it contributes to the authentic development of doctrine. The first law of such development, according to Cardinal Newman, is "preservation of type."[1] In his famous *Essay on the Development of Christian Doctrine,* Newman contends that each doctrine contains its own inner logic and dynamic. A true development consists in the unfolding of these constituent parts, brought to the surface and made explicit by new historical circumstances. In regard to the sacrament of the Anointing of the Sick, for example, Vatican II shifted the principal focus of the sacrament from death and dying to sickness and healing. While such relocation was fully within the scope of authentic development (indeed, the canons of the Council of Trent use the term "Anointing of the Sick" as well as the more familiar "Extreme Unction"), the change in practice was dramatic.[2] Heretofore the appearance of a priest at a sick bed was interpreted as a harbinger of the angel of death, Extreme Unction literally regarded as the "last" sacrament a person was likely to receive.

Mariology provides other examples of the development of doctrine. The doctrines of both the Immaculate Conception and the Assumption unfold what is central to Mary's role in the Gospels, especially in Luke and John, Mary as disciple par excellence and so as the model of discipleship. The Immaculate Conception underscores the radical nature of her call, which penetrates to her very origin as a human person, preserving her from original sin. The Assumption represents the disciple in triumph, brought to perfection in the kingdom. Mary is assumed into heaven as the first of Jesus's followers. Both the Assumption and Immaculate Conception were traditional beliefs. Their definition in the modern era places those ancient beliefs in a new context, adding additional layers of meaning.

The principle of "preservation of type" is open-ended and does not bind the hands of future believers. Yet it is fundamentally a conservative principle that can absorb complimentary but not sharply antithetical differences. In other words, some changes are so radical as to rupture the type, proposing instead a new model. It is clear, for example, from the writings of Martin Luther, John Calvin, and others that the received tradition in regard to sacraments and ministry was not merely reexamined by the reformers with an eye to gradual improvement but was being replaced with new models and new doctrines. True, lines of continuity remained, but the element of discontinuity — the break — was larger.

These general considerations form a necessary backdrop to appreciate the efforts of Vatican II to renew the Catholic doctrine of the priesthood. The focus on doctrine itself deserves a word of explanation. Bernard Lonergan locates *doctrine* on the level of decision-making, *theology* (systematics) on the level of understanding.[3] Theology explores the road ahead, explaining the Gospel and the church's tradition; doctrine consolidates the theological discussion into decisions about the future. A traditional function of theology (but not the only one) is to explain the meaning of church teaching. The focus in what follows is on the interplay between theology and doctrine as the official church makes the critical decisions that set new structures and parameters for the priestly office.

DOCTRINE OF THE PRIESTHOOD
BEFORE VATICAN II

A sense of how doctrines develop helps us to appreciate the weight of a tradition of almost a thousand years about the priesthood in the Roman rite. It also helps us to grasp the large scope of the reforms in the priestly office that Vatican II proposed.

The doctrine of the priesthood that held sway in the Catholic Church in the West focused single-mindedly on the Eucharist. According to its basic tenet, the essence of the priesthood consisted in the power to change bread and wine into the Body and Blood of Christ and to prepare Christians to worthily receive Holy Communion through the sacrament of Penance. The eucharistic focus represented the common view of all major scholastic theologians (Peter Lombard, Thomas Aquinas, Bonaventure, Scotus, and others). Duns Scotus's emphasis on the "two powers," the power to consecrate and the power to forgive sins, eventually became the more common opinion among Catholic theologians after the Reformation.[4] The Decree for the Armenians of the Council of Florence (1439) provided a succinct statement of the church's position prior to the Reformation.[5] This position on the sacrament of Holy Orders was reaffirmed and given firm doctrinal status by the Council of Trent.[6] The *Catechism* of the Council of Trent neatly summarized its teaching.[7]

The crux of the argument among the scholastic theologians, absorbed root and branch into church doctrine, is that the highest and noblest function of a priest was the power to consecrate the Body and Blood of Christ. Nothing can compare with this breathtaking endowment. Hence the fullness of the priesthood must reside in the *priesthood in the presbyteral order* because this was when this unique power was bestowed. (This conviction represented a notable departure from the view of the patristic church, which the Eastern Orthodox Church continued, namely, that the fullness of the priesthood rests in the office of the bishop.)

Center and Periphery

In the centuries following the Reformation, church doctrine on the sacrament of Orders was consistently reaffirmed. *At its center* stood the priesthood. By contrast, the episcopal office remained *at the periphery* in a limbo of open questions.

The *Roman Catechism* provides a convenient guide to the traditional doctrine of the priesthood. It begins with the classic starting point. "For the power of consecrating and offering the body and blood of our Lord and of forgiving sins . . . not only has nothing equal or like to it on earth, but even surpasses human reason and understanding."[8] This singular power, bestowed at priestly ordination, is anchored in the much wider context of four minor orders (porter, reader, exorcist, and acolyte) and three major orders (subdeacon, deacon, and priest). The eucharistic focus is thereby extended in all directions. Neither minor nor major orders have independent status. They are simply stepping stones to the priesthood, ultimately leading to the celebration of the Eucharist. Tonsure marks the beginning of the process, the official entrance into the "clerical state," followed by the reception of minor orders in order of precedence. They start at the back of church (porter, doorkeeper) and lead to the front, to the altar. The last and highest minor order is that of the acolyte, sometimes called the candle-bearer, who serves the major ministers, the deacon and subdeacon.

Major orders begin with the subdiaconate, which, strictly speaking, did not belong to the sacrament even though the most onerous duties of the priesthood, celibacy and the recitation of the breviary, were incurred at that point. The second degree of major orders was the diaconate. The "third and highest degree of all Sacred Orders is the priesthood."[9] Although the priesthood is one, it appears with various degrees of "dignity and power." Under this heading, bishops, archbishops, patriarchs, and finally the pope are ranked.[10] There is no discussion of the "ordination" of bishops and one could not infer from the *Roman Catechism* that the ordination of bishops was included in the sacrament of Orders. The minister of the sacrament of Orders is the bishop. The role of the bishop in regard to the sacrament of Confirmation is couched in similar terms. It leaves open the question of whether in extraordinary circumstances, the power to confirm and, even more significantly, the power to ordain might be delegated to a simple priest.

The *Roman Catechism* continued the standard Western approach concerning the fullness of the priesthood. But by establishing the priesthood within a context of minor and major orders, it also presented a schematic blueprint for seminary formation. The priesthood would be received after an extended period of preparation, marked at each point, first by the reception of tonsure, then by the reception of the minor orders in order of rank, then by the reception of subdiaconate and diaconate. The process culminated in ordination to the priesthood. This tradition predated the Council of Trent. Novel after Trent was the tradition's widespread dissemination as seminary education developed in later centuries.

The Status of the Bishops

There were many questions that the Council of Trent intentionally left undecided, creating a limbo of open questions *at the periphery* surrounding the episcopal office. Did the episcopacy truly belong to the sacrament of Orders or was a bishop simply a priest who was given a special "dignity and power"? Was a bishop's jurisdiction his own or was it a delegated one? In other words, was he simply a kind of regional representative of the Holy See without independent status? If so, did it make sense to speak of a special "order of bishops"? Was a bishop truly "ordained" or was it more accurate to speak of his "consecration," like the consecration of an abbot? Could a simple priest without this "dignity and power" be given special delegation to ordain candidates to the diaconate and the priesthood? In other words, if a simple priest possessed the fullness of the priesthood, was the power to ordain inchoately contained in his office from the start in that extraordinary capacity to change bread and wine into the Body and Blood of Christ? Was it similar to the role of bishop and priest vis-à-vis Confirmation? The bishop is the ordinary minister, the priest, the extraordinary.

However, it would be false to create the impression that these open questions floated in a Sargasso Sea without direction. In reality, they were consigned to the domain of theology, standard grist for the theological manuals of the nineteenth and twentieth centuries. These questions were converted into the "theses" of the manuals, the building blocks of neoscholastic theology. But surely of all of them, the key question was the sacramentality of the episcopacy. Did the episcopacy truly belong to the sacrament of Holy Orders? Following Robert Bellarmine, most authors of theological manuals answered affirmatively. A positive response here also carried a clear drift on other questions. If the bishop's special status came to him by virtue of ordination, it seemed right to speak of the "fullness of priesthood" resting in the episcopal office. It also seemed right to speak about the special collective status of bishops, their existence as a "college of bishops." If bishops were the sole ministers of the sacrament of Orders by right, then such authority could probably not be extended to an ordinary priest.

Summarizing the period from Trent to Vatican II, Kenan Osborne writes that it is fair "to consider Roman Catholic theology on the priesthood as a fairly single entity from the end of the Reformation down to the middle of the twentieth century."[11] Though moving at a glacial pace, doctrinal development led in a single, steady direction on the status of the episcopacy. Pius XII, in the apostolic constitution *Sacramentum Ordinis* (1947), established the matter and form of the diaconate, priesthood, and episcopacy, assuming that all three belonged to the sacrament of Holy Orders.[12] Nevertheless the difficulty remained that this view retained only the status of a "theological opinion" in official parlance, albeit buttressed by firm but varying degrees of authority. Ludwig Ott, writing in 1952, was probably representative. While the sacramentality of the priesthood is described as "Catholic doctrine" (*de fide*), the sacramentality of the episcopacy and diaconate remains only a "certain opinion" (*sententia certa*).[13] Sola in 1962 described the sacramentality of the episcopacy in similar terms. Only rarely was it described as "Catholic doctrine" (*de fide*), for example, in Tanquerey.[14]

In other words, the line between *theological opinion* and *doctrinal decision* had not yet been crossed. The practice also wavered. It was common down to Vatican II to speak of the "consecration" (not the "ordination") of bishops and, truth be told, most bishops thought of themselves first as priests. This represented a fair estimation of their own consciousness because the status of priests was clearer and more firmly fixed, even for bishops.

In one sense, the work of Vatican II on the priesthood represented a continuation of a gradual and consistent development. Indeed, it may be regarded as a parade example of doctrinal development, the return of the Catholic tradition to its patristic roots and to the practice of the Orthodox East. At the same time, the council's action represented a momentous change, a tectonic shift, the realignment of thousand-year tradition in a new direction with many unintended consequences. Vatican II's decisions on the status of priests and bishops was in equal measure an evolutionary development and a revolutionary turn.

A PRIEST BEFORE VATICAN II

What kind of priest did this doctrine — and a thousand-year tradition — produce? George Bernanos and Françcois Mauriac in France and J. F. Powers in the United States, among others, give us memorable portraits of priests. Here is a priest in the 1950s, not memorable, but not untypical either.

Father Richard Finster was regular in just about everything he did. When he said mass, his hands never extended beyond his shoulders and the sign of the cross never went wider than the pall that covered the chalice. He recited the breviary with the same precision, pronouncing each word. He was seldom late for an appointment, never missed a communion call, and went to confession himself once every three weeks. He always wore clerical attire except for his day off. That was regular, too. Eighteen holes of golf, a drink before dinner, and home by nine. He visited his family almost every week and while his brothers called him Dick, his mother always called him "Father," both to his face and when she talked about him. He had priest-friends who were more raucous, but that was not his way.

What else did you expect? He entered the seminary at thirteen and was ordained at twenty-five. The clerical role was grafted directly onto his personality in its most formative years. He was literally encased in the priesthood. Was there another personality under all those regular priestly ways? Who could say? But that was certainly not his or anyone else's question in those days.

THE DOCTRINE OF THE PRIESTHOOD
ACCORDING TO VATICAN II

Vatican II made two major contributions to the church's understanding of the priesthood. First, it offered a new doctrinal interpretation of the priesthood. Second, by elevating what heretofore had been a firmly grounded *theological opinion* to the status of *official doctrine,* the council formally taught that "the fullness of the priesthood" rested in the office of the bishop. It thereby set a new benchmark for all future discussion of ordained ministry in the Catholic Church.

The New Interpretation

The dogmatic constitution *Lumen Gentium* locates the subject of hierarchy, laity, and religious within a wider vision of the mystery of the Trinity. "The mystery of the holy Church is already brought to light in the way it was founded. For the Lord Jesus inaugurated his church by preaching the Good News." Rising from the dead, he was constituted as "Lord, the Christ, and as Priest for ever."[15] The inner nature of the church is revealed in the various images used to describe it: a sheepfold, a cultivated field, the building of God, the New Jerusalem, the Body of Christ.

Beneath these metaphorical riches, three connecting links hold the Constitution on the Church together and join it to other council documents, especially those on bishops and priests. As prophet, priest, and king — the *tria munera,* or three offices — Christ bequeathed to the people of God as a whole a threefold task that constitutes the church's essence and its fundamental mission: preaching, sanctifying, and shepherding. This threefold legacy of Christ to the church established the larger framework within which both the priesthood of the faithful and the ministerial priesthood could be located and interpreted.

The first mention of the priesthood in *Lumen Gentium* states,

Though they differ essentially and not only in degree, the common priesthood of the faithful and the ministerial or hierarchical priesthood are none the less ordered one to another; each in its own proper way shares in the one priesthood of

Christ. The ministerial priest, by the sacred power that he has, forms and rules the priestly people; in the person of Christ he effects the eucharistic sacrifice and offers to God in the name of all the people. The faithful indeed, by virtue of their royal priesthood, participate in the offering of the Eucharist.[16]

Likewise the prophetic and royal offices of Christ are given to the church as a whole prior to the distribution of roles among hierarchy and laity. The laity "in their own way share the priestly, prophetic and kingly office of Christ."[17] What distinguishes the laity is its *secular* character; its principal field of endeavor is *the world.* The hierarchy assume primary responsibility for preaching, sanctifying, and shepherding *within the church.* The new context is not simple and such a division of labor does not answer all implicit questions, regarding, for example, the responsibilities of the laity within the church.

However, the chief concern here is the way in which the new context shifts the definition of the priesthood. By beginning with the Christological foundation of church, the traditional eucharistic focus is retained but broadened and thereby transformed. In other words, as the threefold office of Christ as prophet, priest, and king steps to the fore, the Tridentine focus on the power to consecrate and the power to forgive sins remains, but moves to the side. The threefold office of Christ also connects more closely the Christological *and* the ecclesiological dimensions of the priesthood, both of which are essential. The priest acts *in persona Christi;* but he also acts in the name of the whole people of God, the church.

At every point, the church's traditional understanding of the priesthood is broadened. The first task of priests, preaching, belongs to his prophetic function.[18] The word must be preached before it can be celebrated and practiced. This emphasis reflects the impact of the Catholic Church's recovery of its biblical heritage, an element on clear display in the reform of the liturgy and here as well in the new interpretation of the priesthood. From a historical perspective, this was a bold stroke. The Constitution on the Liturgy proclaims that liturgy of word and sacrament "form one single act of worship."[19] In highlighting the role of the word at the Eucharist and the importance of preaching, the priest's role as minister of the word takes on new importance. This represents a fresh emphasis in the church's doctrinal interpretation of the priesthood.[20]

Priest as priest, as sacramental minister, is the second of the three offices of Christ. In one sense, this is the traditional Catholic emphasis. But even here the priestly role is transformed. The Constitution on the Liturgy did nothing less than order a major overhaul of the church's worship, of the Eucharist, of the other sacraments, and of the sacramental rites. If the priest was traditionally the minister of the sacraments, these reforms gave him an entirely new script. Everywhere his lines were changed, and it all transpired swiftly. In other words, it was not as if the traditional role of the priest as priest was left standing but now flanked by two additions, the prophetic and shepherding roles. On the contrary, the traditional role of priest as sacramental minister was no less transformed.

The third role, priest as king or shepherd barely needed justification for its formal inclusion in a new interpretation of the priesthood. Shepherding is a principal task of priests, certainly of diocesan priests, essential by any measure to the actual function of a priest. Diocesan priests would describe themselves primarily in these terms.

These three roles (prophet, priest, and king) and the tasks they generate (preaching, sanctifying, and shepherding) run through the entire church and through all ranks of ministers, although with varying degrees of authority and responsibility. They set the master plan for Christ's church and the great tasks that join the pope, bishops, priests, deacons, and laity in their endeavors. They therefore possess a vertical and hierarchical dimension. But the inclusion of the laity in the prophetic, sanctifying, and governing tasks of the church also created movement in the other direction. A sense of horizontal co-responsibility for the welfare of Christ's church joins all the faithful by virtue of their baptism.

It is sometimes said that the council affirmed the priesthood of the faithful and the ministerial priesthood without defining how the two relate to each other, and this may be a fair observation.

While greater specificity is always helpful, it can hardly be a concern here to see a blurring of priestly identity in a thousand-year tradition that has relentlessly affirmed the uniqueness of the priesthood. It seems proper to see the Tridentine formula as emphasizing the *specific difference* of the ministerial priesthood, while Vatican II stresses the *common denominator* that join all ranks of ministers. In other words, the church does not annul older doctrinal definitions; it places them in new contexts that shift their meanings in new directions.

The Bishop, the Fullness of the Priesthood

The priest to whom *Lumen Gentium* first refers in paragraph 10 is, above all, the bishop, and this introduces the second major contribution of Vatican II. By an action of the ordinary magisterium, the council declared that the "fullness of the priesthood" rests in the office of the bishop. This now became official church teaching. The relevant section of the Constitution on the Church is explicit in its intention.

> This holy synod teaches, moreover, that the fullness of the sacrament of Orders is conferred by episcopal consecration, that fullness, namely, which both in the liturgical tradition of the Church and in the language of the Fathers of the Church is called the high priesthood, the acme of the sacred ministry. Now, episcopal consecration confers, together with the office of sanctifying, the duty also of teaching and ruling, which, however, of their very nature can be exercised only in hierarchical communion with the head and members of the college.[21]

By any measure, this was a momentous decision that shifted the center of gravity of the priesthood. However, the decision was not made without reference to the future direction of other ranks of ordained ministers. *Lumen Gentium* devotes a paragraph to the priesthood and one to the diaconate.[22] These sections together enable the Constitution on the Church to sketch out a new blueprint for ordained ministry, which the *Catechism of the Catholic Church* of 1992 could summarize in the way the *Roman Catechism* set forth the teaching of the Council of Trent.

Each of the ranks of ordained ministry — bishops, priests, and deacons — constitute a distinct ordo, or group. Ordained ministry, then, is never an individual but always a collegial undertaking. The bishops form a college, headed by the pope, whose concern is the church universal. Priests form a college, called a presbyterium, headed by the bishop, whose focus is the local church. Deacons also form an ordo headed by the bishop. By virtue of ordination, priests in the presbyteral order possess the dignity of the priesthood of Jesus Christ in their own right. While diaconate is conferred by the sacrament of Orders, it carries a sharing in ministry but not in the priesthood.[23]

While *Lumen Gentium* sketched a broad blueprint for the three ranks of ordained ministry, it did not complete a specific one for priesthood in the presbyteral order. This task was left to the apostolic letters *Ministeria Quaedam* (On Lector and Acolyte) and *Ad Pascendum* (Norms for Diaconate) of 1972. In *Ad Pascendum,* the council's decision to detach the diaconate from its previous setting as the final stepping-stone to the priesthood was implemented. Instead, the diaconate was established as an independent ministerial rank. *Ministeria Quaedam* followed a similar plan for lector and acolyte. They were no longer to be called "minor orders" or viewed as steps to the priesthood. They were now to be called "ministries" into which candidates were "installed," not ordained. They were now to be regarded as *lay ministries,* which gave expression to the council's desire that all the faithful be led to that full, conscious, and active participation in the liturgy that is theirs by virtue of baptism.

By a stroke of the pen, the apostolic letters radically reshaped an earlier blueprint for priesthood in the presbyteral order largely by way of excision. As lector and acolyte were established as lay ministries, tonsure, the minor orders, and the subdiaconate were suppressed in the Latin rite. Instead, a candidate for the priesthood entered the clerical state first at diaconate. A new rite for the admission of candidates to diaconate/priesthood was introduced in which the candidate publicly declares his intention to aspire to sacred orders and the church formally acknowledges his declaration. Candidates for diaconate/priesthood were also to be installed in the ministries of lector and acolyte; these, however, were no longer regarded as steps to the priesthood but as lay ministries that candidates, still laymen themselves, appropriately received.

THE NEW BREED

Did the changes at Vatican II give birth to a new kind of priest? So it was said at the time. They were called the "new breed." The phrase now carries a whiff of the 1970s. But new priests did seem different after the council.

Take Father "Pat." That's what everyone called him. He was in the seminary for three years, spent a half year in an internship in an inner city parish, and then was ordained. Pat wore an open-collared clerical shirt, with well-worn jeans. De rigeur for the time, he played the guitar. But more than that, he had something very "natural" about him. He had an easy way of celebrating mass, was able to improvise and throw in a joke or two, and had a great way with teenagers. He told them how important it was to "get in touch with yourself." But some ladies of the Legion of Mary were skeptical. That was until he presided at May devotions. He composed a song about the mysteries of the rosary, "Mary, Why Are You Weeping?" which he sang in a soft tenor voice. Each week he added a new verse. By the end of May the church was packed. The doubts dissolved.

His pastor, on the other hand, Father Finster, seemed increasingly out of step with the time. What was normal in the 1950s, now seemed downright rigid. The pastor liked Father Pat. Who couldn't? But he looked at him as across a species gap, the way humans view gorillas at the zoo. However, he had one insight into Father Pat that was on the money. Pat was a child of his time. If Father Finster was a priest of the 1950s, Father Pat was wrapped up in the 1970s. Priestly formation had barely grazed the surface. It also became clear why Pat talked so often about getting in touch with one's self. Surface impressions to the contrary, Pat was just finding out who he was. He took advantage of the new postconciliar freedom and left the priesthood after four years. It is probably closer to the truth to

*see Father Pat as a late-bloomer in a roman collar. He really wanted
to be a lawyer. But he looked back on his career in the priesthood
fondly, as a young man in the 1970s might view a stint in the Peace
Corps.*

Taking Stock

Acting under the inspiration of the Holy Spirit and on the advice of
the best theological minds of the age, Vatican II gave the ordinary
priesthood a considerable jolt. When the reforms of Vatican II are
viewed together, it is fair to say that they firmly shifted the bearings
of a thousand-year tradition on multiple fronts. That is comparable
to the shift of a tectonic plate deeply buried along an extended fault
line. The actual surface slippage may seem to have been slight at
first, but inexplicable ruptures, bursts from subterranean fissures,
suddenly appeared, much to everyone's surprise. No one expected,
for example, the dramatic downturn in vocations to the priesthood
in the United States from 1967 to 1980, which was remarkable by
any measure. Even more surprisingly, no one foresaw that priests
would leave the active ministry in such large numbers in the immediate wake of a great ecumenical council whose reforms were
greeted with so much enthusiasm and such a sense of hope. No one
suspected that some of the priests who remained were so damaged
personally. The unavoidable conclusion is that after the council the
priesthood in the presbyteral order entered a period of considerable
disorientation that no one foresaw or expected.

It may have been that the *postconciliar* priesthood was a victim of its *preconciliar* success. The priesthood before the council
was highly respected worldwide with vocations on the upswing in
many countries, universally regarded as the stable and dependable
workhorse of the church's pastoral efforts. Who could envision that
such a stable ministry would experience such instability in the postconciliar years? But now at a distance of almost two generations,
the reasons become somewhat clearer.

Vatican II was a celebration of the importance and the dignity
of the episcopal office, a signal achievement of the council. Individually, the bishops represented the fullness of the priesthood.

Collectively, the college of bishops was co-responsible with the pope for the welfare of the universal church. Their collective authority for the regional church was also enhanced. At the other end of the spectrum, the importance of the whole people of God by virtue of their baptism was recognized both in *Lumen Gentium* and in the Constitution on the Liturgy.

The priesthood in the presbyteral order seemed a diminished participant in the new scheme of things. In addition, large portions of what had been components of the priesthood were simply peeled off without much thought as to the consequences. In every case a legitimate *functional* or *practical* consideration was accompanied by a *symbolic* consequence for the priesthood. Did it make any real difference if tonsure, the minor orders, or subdiaconate were abolished? Did it not make good sense to establish lay ministries to replace from the minor orders? Did it not it make practical sense to open the diaconate to married men? The answer in every case is yes. But the symbolic consequences on the priesthood were enormous. It was not just that a very long tradition of minor and major orders was eliminated. It seemed that the underlying wisdom of that tradition was disparaged as well. The old wisdom said that it was important to approach the priesthood in small, gradual steps, that priestly formation should encompass a long period of preparation, marked by official acknowledgments along the way.

When these factors are added together, they spell the symbolic diminishment of the priesthood in the presbyteral order. So, as the accomplishments of the council were trumpeted, the drumbeat of diminishment was loud enough to bring vocations tumbling and to discourage large numbers of priests from continuing in their vocation. The priesthood that entered the council with a full bank account had been subject to heavy symbolic withdrawals. No new deposits or depositors were on the horizon.

The diminishment was not only symbolic. In spite of the new agenda that the council served up for the clergy, the training of priests immediately after the council was often reduced to a three-year in-house program followed by a brief internship in a parish. This was Father Pat's priestly formation. As tonsure and the minor orders were dropped, the Rite of Candidacy was introduced after

1972 as the sole step prior to entering the diaconate/priesthood. It is hard to imagine a less inspiring liturgical rite, all words, no symbols, over in a trice. It prompted one woman to ask, "Is that all there is?"

Recent history also carries the story of a turnaround. Seminary education stands on the verge of its third set of visitations, but the progress should not be overlooked in light of recent events. Priests ordained in the last twenty years have become increasingly more stable and dependable, and that fact will become evident. As to an authentic "new breed" of priest, it will take four or five generations to produce one. It is said that in Bach's choral music the Reformation finally found its own authentic voice, many generations after the fact. The comparison is apt for a vocation as old as the Roman Catholic priesthood. This is only the beginning.

A Final Balance

The starting point of a profitable assessment of Vatican II's reform of the priesthood should be Karl Rahner's interpretation.[24] Why a great reform council in a time of peace and prosperity? Rahner's answer: to prepare the church for the transition from a Western church to a truly world church. Rahner's underlying assumption underscores our point. Vatican II was meant to prepare the church for the *future*. Yes, for a world church, but even more for the new millennium that opened on September 11, 2001. The council's reforms for ordained ministry — bishop, priest, and deacon — must be viewed in the same light. The scope of the new blueprint is large and will take many generations to come to fruition. That assumption itself constitutes an act of faith and must form the backdrop for our own partial judgments after forty years.

Nevertheless, the recent scandals and consequent loss of credibility of bishops and priests draw a line in the sand. They force a more definite assessment of the position to date. They round off a forty-year period and ask for a balance in simple terms. Eugen Rosenstock-Huessy wrote that every revolution must undergo the humiliation of its own ideals before it can stand upright before the bar of history.[25] The ideals of the French Revolution, for example, were dealt a slight by the Revolution of 1830 and Louis

Philippe's slogan, *Enrichissez-vous:* the French middle-class should now be more concerned with wealth than freedom.[26] The recent sexual abuse scandals represent nothing less than a great moment of testing for priests and bishops alike, and for the priesthood that emerged from Vatican II.

What people do in such moments is to reach for their deepest spiritual roots, hoping to regain courage and strength. They seek to reform themselves. But what of the corporate, public endeavor of the priesthood? The view attributed to the old Austrian bureaucracy — that everything would settle itself in the end if one waited long enough — does not seem good advice here.[27] Better is an example closer to home, the Third Plenary Council of Baltimore, which dealt extensively with priestly formation. While not without its limitations, it represented a vigorous, public step toward addressing the future of the priesthood.[28]

For the individual priest at this time, the path is also clear. In a time of testing, immerse yourself ever more deeply in the mystery of Christ whom you represent and in whose name you act.

Chapter Nine

THE THEOLOGY OF
THE PRIESTHOOD

I F THERE IS but one priesthood, that of Jesus Christ, the person of Christ is always the measure. If the priest acts in *persona Christi*, head of the church, and in the name of the whole people of God, Christ must constitute the starting point for any and every theological reflection on the fundamental meaning of the priesthood.

JESUS CHRIST

The sixth-century encaustic icon of Christ Pantocrator from St. Catherine's monastery in the Sinai gives striking expression to this starting point. The claim is made that this is perhaps the oldest attempt at a portrait of Jesus. For sure, it is unique. It has dispensed with the stylized features associated with icons and is much closer to the actual picture of a single individual, the eyes not quite even. This is why it is so special. It gives graphic expression to the central truth of the faith. Christians believe that a little over two thousand years ago, the Lord God appeared in their midst in a specific human person, one like themselves, with a human mind and a human will, a human body and a human soul.

All those elements were points of controversy and objects of definition in the early church. This was to secure the fact, so simple and so revolutionary, that slips so easily from us. The Word became flesh and dwelt among us. The Christ was like us in all things save sin. Philosophers, Hegel among them, saw a progression toward the Incarnation. In Egypt, the gods appeared as animals; in Greece, as playful, sometimes capricious humans. But among the Jews was the claim first made that God came to earth in the form of a single, actual man. Von Balthasar captures the point in a striking metaphor. Two thousand years ago, he writes, a giant meteor struck the planet, and whether subsequent ages believe in him or not, the enormous crater that the single person of Jesus Christ gouged in this earth remains behind for all to see and to ponder.[1]

The relative ease — without underestimating the difficulties — with which an originally Jewish message about Jesus was preached in a Gentile setting is itself striking. The universal implications of the revelation of God in Jesus Christ were apparent almost at once. In fact, they became clearer in their new context. Not only Jews longed for salvation but Gentiles as well, indeed all people who share the human condition. The figure of the "Christ" speaks a universal human language because it speaks to a universal human longing. For that reason, all people have understood almost at once the claim the Gospel made.

It can be simply put. In a single human life, all the goodness, the potential for noble purpose, the capacity for right conduct of which all people feel themselves capable, once and just once, was fulfilled. To one degree or another, everyone feels this potential as part of the human condition. But it appears usually as empty warehouse space, unused potential or wasted talent. It is felt largely as absence or pain. Indeed, this awareness is the source of that special misery unique to the human lot. People feel that potential within themselves, feel that they could be better, finer, nobler than they are, but experience quickly teaches them otherwise. They seldom realize a hundredth part of what they might be.

They also feel that something is wrong with themselves and with the world. It is sometimes argued that the doctrine of original sin is the most practically demonstrable Christian belief, hardly an object of faith but of simple observation. The quarrel is with the source of the difficulty. Is society the source of human woe as Rousseau argued (whose teaching Western civilization largely followed)? Or does the malady go deeper? Can humans cure it themselves or is the solution beyond them? The current mantra that urges all people to "feel good about themselves" only underscores the universal inability to do so. Indeed, the seeds of perfection within the human heart often act like the proverbial pebble in the shoe, a special source of unhappiness, because they serve as a steady reminder of standards no one ever reaches.

Still, the memory of wholeness is haunting and it lingers. Most people wonder from time to time if they are pieces of a mosaic that was perhaps once whole, slivers of a mirror now shattered, but once intact. The Gospel says, *it once was so.* The picture one intuits and hopes for once came together in Jesus's life, and his existence is a message from God to all of us. He is God's messenger, who in his person constitutes the message. What better way for God to communicate? Would a book or a letter or a sacred cat have been better? The universe seems to move by its own mysterious and intricate logic; quarks may have revelation enough. But humans, for whom, in Pascal's words, everything is "partly true, partly false" need a special light.[2] Doesn't it make compelling human sense that when God chose to speak, he could do so in no more eloquent, convincing, and intelligible form than through the grammar of a human life lived nobly from start to finish?

Jesus's final destiny introduces the other side of the Christian equation. All the ancient confessions of faith emphasize that Jesus died a human death for the sake of our sins. His death was not staged and it was not peripheral. Indeed, in the oldest account in Mark's Gospel, the story of Jesus's passion and death, the last seven days of his life, occupies fully a third of the narrative. And this is finally to underscore Mark's great climax that only in Jesus's agonizing death on the cross is his divinity fully revealed. Recall the words of the centurion as Jesus dies, "Truly this was the Son of God!" (Mark 15:39)

Jesus took on himself a human death and everything that death symbolizes in life. John Paul II frequently alludes to a culture of death, the shadowy underside of a culture of life. It is a thread that runs throughout the fabric of human life, tying so much human misery into a single package. Death signifies all those things that destroy life that is of human making, in which people are the perpetrators of their own downfall, the legacy of sins large and small. It also signifies everything that destroys life that are not of human making, for which no one is responsible and of which we are all victims, the legacy of human finitude, weakness, sickness, and the random spin of the wheel that brings chance accident and ruin. Jesus took on a human death in all of its dark amplitude and, in so doing, drank the cup of the human condition to its final dregs.

Again, we see the piercing clarity of Mark's insight. He connects Jesus's cry of dereliction, "My God, my God, why have you forsaken me?" (Mark 15:34) to the centurion's confession of faith. Together, they attest that no part of human life remains untouched. No dark niche in the human heart remains that God's love cannot penetrate. It is utterly fitting that in the depth of his suffering and death, Jesus's divine sonship is revealed and proclaimed. Where else in the world is it so desperately needed? Jesus's divinity shines forth in the depth of his suffering and death because God's love has penetrated the human condition so deeply. There is literally no place to hide from such love.

Christians who believe in Jesus Christ, Lord and God, receive an answer to many lingering questions that all people have had. Why were human beings constructed in the peculiar way in which they come? Why do they have so many hopes, longings, and desires far beyond their capacity to ever satisfy them? Were they ultimately made for their own final frustration, nature's great accidental joke on itself? Or were they given a richer, deeper destiny, first fulfilled in Christ, the first of many brothers and sisters, a gift passed on to others? Were the seeds of perfection sown in the human heart — while they may alternately encourage and bedevil us in this life — ultimately meant to truly bloom in the life to come, in the kingdom into which Jesus leads his followers? May one fully believe in and hope for the best and most noble aspirations that God has planted in the human heart?

At the resurrection, Jesus's victory over death was passed on to his followers in a language they could understand. To those who denied and abandoned him, he forgave their sins and infidelities and so bestowed the gift of new life in this life. Certainly the resurrection was never understood as an individual occurrence that happened to Jesus alone. Rather it meant that he had gone ahead into his kingdom and his followers were shortly to follow. For them it seemed as if at Jesus's death the shell of his individual life was cracked open and his spirit was literally inserted into this world, first on his closest followers.[3] Suddenly they began to act less like themselves and more like Jesus, with more boldness and courage, his spirit now intermingled with theirs. Whatever was in Jesus that made him so immeasurably better and nobler than his followers could ever imagine themselves to be was now given to them, his spirit passing through his death and resurrection into the hearts of his followers.

It was also a divine spirit from above, not something this world could produce on its own. In the face of hatred and violence, the spirit that raised Jesus from the dead brought forth the very opposite emotions from those that caused his death, courage with peace and forgiveness for those who had betrayed and persecuted him. The circle of violence that killed the innocent Jesus was broken. Something new had entered the world.[4]

God's revelation in Jesus Christ fulfills but far surpasses human nature. In effect, the *novum* is not finally about us, but about God. Christ, the Incarnate Word, is the opening door to the Triune God in whose divine life the church is founded and endowed, as *Lumen Gentium* wrote.

THE CHURCH

When the first descriptions of the church appear, they bring with them a dazzling reversal. If Jesus is the *single* human person in whom the Word was made flesh, by his resurrection he becomes a *zone of personal presence.* This describes the church at its core. The church is called the Body of Christ in Romans and 1 Corinthians, the place where Jesus's new corporate presence dwells, manifesting itself in the gifts that abound in the Christian community. Christ's Spirit makes Christians into new persons individually and collectively. It makes them into the Body of Christ. Ephesians universalizes the image, adding the distinction between Head and Body. Christ is the heavenly head of the church that is his body, his earthly extension in time.

Cardinal Newman said that if Christians truly believe in the Incarnation, it follows that God would make sure his presence in Christ would continue in time.[5] It would make sense that a church would be part of God's original design. Therefore it is no great leap to believe in the church, once the initial act of faith to believe in Christ has been made. Newman's point may also be verified on an experiential level. The church remains the place where Christ's presence meets his followers.

The Priesthood

The presence of Christ in the church, the priesthood of Jesus Christ, sets the context for the priesthood in all its forms.

The Constitution on the Liturgy discussed the several presences of Christ in the church.[6] When it first appeared, it caused some stir among Catholics. In the past Christ's real presence in the Eucharist was understood against the background of his virtual absence elsewhere. The Constitution on the Liturgy righted the balance. In doing so, it went back to the oldest Christian tradition about the church's heart and center. The church is literally suffused with the presence of Christ. Paul's admonition in 1 Corinthians therefore bears repetition. These various presences are like the limbs of a coordinated body. They flow from a single source, Jesus Christ. They are meant for a single end, to nourish the common good, the presence of Christ in the hearts of the faithful. The similarities and differences between Paul and Vatican II are also striking. The differences are the two thousand years of tradition that came after Paul, a period of complex doctrinal development on many fronts. The similarities are in the continuous efforts to embody Christ's presence in word and sacrament. And in some respects, like the Lord's presence in prayer, there are no differences. The church today remains as it was when it began.

According to the Constitution on the Liturgy, Christ is present when people gather to pray in his name. Christ dwells and acts in their spirit and between their spirits when the church gathers in prayer. Christ is present as the author of the sacraments that touch his followers in a special way at different moments of their lives. Christ is present in the word of God, "since it is he himself who speaks when the holy scriptures are read in the Church." Christ is "present in the Sacrifice of the Mass not only in the person of his minister but especially in the Eucharistic species."[7] The Eucharist is the most intimate and encompassing of the many presences of Christ. In the Eucharist, Christ gives us his own flesh and blood, his life commingled with ours as food for the journey.

Christ is present in the priest. While this presence is inseparable from the other forms of presence, it is unique in its own way. Christ was a single person. It makes sense that he would continue to be represented by individual persons of his choosing. Priests are such people, walking symbols of Christ's presence. They are designated human prisms whose function at any one time does not capture or exhaust a hundredth part of what they symbolize.

As walking symbols of Christ, they join distinguished company. Matthew 25 speaks of Christ's presence in the hungry, the thirsty, the naked, those in prison. Christians acknowledge or deny the presence of Christ by their care for the least of their brothers and sisters. These opportunities take place with some frequency. According to Matthew, they form the basis for God's final judgment as he separates the sheep from the goats at the end of time.

CHRIST'S PRESENCE IN THE CHURCH

The person of Jesus is what the church offers in its most transparent moments. There are theoretical philosophical and theological answers to the human predicament which the tradition offers. But in the thick of things, such answers ring hollow. They make one think of Elaine May's great line, "I love moral problems so much more than real ones."[8] *Why do bad things happen to good people? Who knows for sure? If you are a good person who has just met a calamitous event, abstract answers are thin soup. But the presence of Christ is not. When bad things happen to good people, Jesus is with them. He is always with the victims, close by their side. He has been there himself. Why do well-intentioned people do so many dumb things? Who knows? But they certainly do them, over and over again. Here, too, Jesus is with good people who do foolish things. His presence meant forgiveness to the wrong and thoughtless actions of his followers. And in his life he showed a special love for the sinners and the outcasts, the foolish of this world. In the last analysis, this is the only answer the church has to offer. But Christ's presence is answer enough. Certainly, it is the only thing a priest has to offer.*

THE THREEFOLD OFFICES OF CHRIST

Christ's presence in the church and in the priest is further specified by the threefold office of prophet, priest, and king. These are roles of mediation between God and the human family that developed in Israel's history and were taken over by Christian tradition.

In joining these three offices to describe the person of Christ, the theological lens is opened as wide as possible, its categories stretched to the limits and then overlapped. The intention is to fuse together the most encompassing human categories to grasp what it means to say that the Word became flesh, to understand from the earthly side this gesture of mediation that God himself has initiated. In turn, these three roles generate the great tasks that constitute the church's mission: preaching, sanctifying, and shepherding. Almost from the beginning, the offices of bishop and priest have assumed special responsibilities for these tasks.

When the threefold offices of Christ are applied to the specific role of the priest, another unique perspective appears. In classic terms, prophet, priest, and shepherd constitute a set of offices that describe the deepest point of the priesthood, the *ontic* connection between the priest and the person of Christ. The same set of terms also captures the *functional* nature of the priesthood, what priests actually *do* in their ministry. It is remarkable that one set of categories can describe both *depth* and *surface, functional* and *ontic* connection.

In reality, this interplay reveals a more encompassing logic, primitive and dynamic, that has characterized church office almost from the start. It manifests itself in the first turn the office of presbyter-bishop underwent in its development. Originally, the presbyter-bishops of the pastoral letters of Timothy and Titus are given a *functional* rationale. Stewardship in the church calls for a sober, commonsense person who can manage his own household, one who does not get drunk and will not steal, a kind of first-century Rotarian. However, about the year 100 in the letters of Ignatius of

Antioch, the bishop is intimately linked to the Eucharist, and here a striking identification is made. The church's deepest inner source of unity, the *Eucharist,* is identified with its most visible, external symbol, the office of *bishop.* The community then needs a personified symbol of its encompassing unity that goes from top to bottom, from *inner source* to *outer expression.* As the various levels of unity in the church appear, the same need for a symbol and agent of unity is felt. As the regional church emerges, the office of patriarch appears. As the universal church grows into a historical reality, the office of pope emerges as its center.[9] Each level of unity has a corresponding symbol and agent of the church's oneness. Yet how are these complex levels of unity and their corresponding relationships reconciled one with another? The matter is never argued or explained. The mystery is assumed: the church is one.

THE MARKS OF THE CHURCH

The marks of the church overlap and interrelate in complex ways. That the church is one is a characteristic of its public life; such unity is grounded in its second mark, holiness, a quality of depth. The church as Catholic is the mark of its universality, which, in turn, is rooted in the faith of the apostles, a characteristic of historical origins.

The church does not possess these marks on its own. They are gifts of Christ. "It is Christ who, through the Holy Spirit, makes the church one, holy, catholic and apostolic, and it is he who calls her to realize each of these qualities."[10] These gifts come to full realization only in the kingdom. In history, the interplay between surface and depth, light and darkness, revelation and hiddenness characterize the church's life. The visibility of these marks is only partial, but their manifestations are significant. They constitute, according to Vatican I's *Dei Filius* "a great and perpetual motive of credibility and an irrefutable witness of her mission."[11] In other words, they serve as beacons, indicating that the church is on course toward its final destination.

If these marks are essential characteristics of the church and its mission, they must relate to the priesthood as well. In fact, these marks must also be defining characteristics of the priest. If the tasks of preaching, sanctifying, and shepherding are entrusted to those who publicly represent Christ in a special way, by the same token those same persons must be symbols and agents of the church's unity, holiness, catholicity, and apostolic origins. If preaching, sanctifying, and shepherding are the *tasks*, the marks provide a *sense of mission*. Their historical manifestations are signs to believer and unbeliever alike that the church is on course because its defining characteristics are visible. This is why they can function as motives of credibility. Likewise, these marks can be lost. But their continuing historical absence constitutes a witness against the church, indeed a scandal.

The marks of the church must be distinguishing characteristics of priests as walking symbols of Christ's presence: here doctrine leads to theology and spirituality in a straight line. Yet the marks of the church as they relate to priests comprise less a set of skills than of personal qualities. These qualities flow from that deeper source of authority called *character* and are immediately evident, particularly in regard to the first two marks. Priests as symbols and agents of the church's unity, its holiness, its catholic and apostolic character bear special responsibility for keeping these marks visible. Both their successes and failures are as visible as the marks themselves.

Priest as Symbol and Agent of Unity

The first mark of the church is unity. The church is one. All levels of communion in the church assume collaborative relationships whose first task is to make sure the unity of the church is tangible, palpable, and alive. This unity has always been a complex one, a unity in diversity — no surprise for those who adore a Triune God, one in Nature, three in Persons. Maintaining such unity is a paramount challenge for church ministry in all forms and for priests and bishops in particular. They function like the center of a wheel from which spokes extend in all directions. The analogy applies both to the pastor of a parish and, even more, the bishop of a diocese.

Clearly there are human and spiritual qualities that help or hinder a priest or a bishop in fulfilling such a role. Anger and hostility, for example, almost by definition, separate and divide people and are poor qualities for effective church ministers. The higher one ascends the hierarchical ladder, the more damaging such qualities become. If bishops and priests are symbols and agents of the church's unity, they themselves must be like magnets that draw people and hold them together. They must literally become *sym-bolon,* people who tie things together, able to call people to a wider sense of community that transcends personal self-interest. Their best efforts are devoted to calling down the *koinonia,* the communion of the Holy Spirit, the real force that joins people to one another. This communion is not a gift from above that drops down vertically and stops. Rather it becomes a circling bond of charity that joins Christians to one another as it unites them to Christ. The gift makes them larger than themselves individually and collectively, a whole that is much more than the sum of its parts.

Christian communities have always come in odd sizes and shapes. A Christian community is enriched by the diversity it can absorb. Still, how many differences can any community absorb without sundering its unity? Pascal describes the alternatives: "Multiplicity which is not reduced to unity is confusion. Unity which does not depend on multiplicity is tyranny."[12] Priests and bishops are called to be ministers who foster the unity of the church. As symbols and agents of unity, they fulfill this role by constantly balancing unity and diversity in the parish and in a diocese.

TWO AGENTS OF THE CHURCH'S UNITY

Every parish they sent Father Smith to began to fall apart. Whatever quarrels had been slumbering between the Legion of Mary and the St. Vincent de Paul Society were reawakened. The director of religious education and the liturgy director were now at odds. The finance committee was feuding with the parish council. How did he do it? God knows, but he did it every time. An angry man himself, he was like a lightning rod; he drew conflict to himself and then dispersed it to those around him, putting people at odds with one another. When he left a parish, people invariably heaved a collective sigh of relief.

Father Jones was the kind of person the diocese sent in when someone like Father Smith left. He wasn't particularly intelligent, nor an especially good preacher. But he was a good listener, he didn't take sides, and he knew how to cobble out practical solutions that satisfied most people. Above all, he was a peaceful man who was respectful of others. Whatever troubled situation he entered quickly began to settle down. People always wanted him to stay.

Priest as Symbol and Agent of Holiness

The second mark of the church is holiness. Priests are called to be symbols and agents of the church's holiness. Since God alone is holy, the goal is to make the church *transparent* to the presence of God, to let the sacramental nature of the church shine forth. Just as Christ is the sacrament of encounter with God, so the church must be the sacrament of Christ's presence within the human family.

What fosters the holiness of the church? This is a special challenge for Catholics who have a deep and abiding faith in the sacramentality of material objects, churches, statues, paintings, relics, vestments, and sacred vessels. But at times those objects no longer point to Christ's presence but obscure it. Old buildings, for example, quickly point to big dollars, to problems of deferred maintenance, to earthly baggage accumulated along the way that is best discarded. The same question can be asked about church organization. When does middle-management lose a sense of transparency to the church's mission and instead become an end in itself?

The largest obstacle to holiness is sin, and though the church may be holy, its members often are not. But by the same token, because they are sinners, the church's holiness does not remain an abstraction to them. They encounter it in the forgiveness of their sins. They also can see it on occasion in the holiness of others. How much difference one holy person makes, one person who seems transparent to God's presence! Is there any more adequate sacramental vessel, a monstrance of God's presence, than a human personality suffused with the love of God? Is there anything more riveting, more justifying of the church's existence than a single person in whom holiness of life has found a home? When such a person appears, everyone thinks, "This is the reason the church exists." Isn't this true of a priest as well? And isn't the absence of such holiness also notable?

TWO AGENTS OF THE CHURCH'S HOLINESS

Father Tim was a genuinely religious man, that was clear. People often saw him in church praying, never ostentatiously, simply there. Even more, you could hear it in the note of conviction when he preached. He wanted to promote the prayer life of the parish and, no surprise, his interest had an effect. Prayer groups of different kinds sprang up. But it was the general tone he set that really made a difference. It just seemed like a more prayerful place and, as a consequence, people seemed a bit more concerned about one another. A religious man himself, Father Tim brought out the same quality in others.

The woman cursed herself for even thinking it, but she often wondered if Father Tom really believed anything. There was something so mechanical and perfunctory about the way he said mass and preached, a sacramental functionary going through the motions. He sounded unconvinced — better, unconcerned — and was therefore unconvincing. But she knew what he did like — two stiff Manhattans and a sirloin steak. He was to her the embodiment of the old saying, "If you go to a strange town and want to know a good restaurant, ask the local priest. He always knows the places." It was okay for her; she was brought up Catholic. But would a man like that be able to keep her kids coming to church? She thought not.

Priest as Symbol and Agent of the Church's Catholicity

The church is Catholic. For the first time in its long history, the universality of the Catholic Church has become a tangible reality, with local churches burgeoning on every continent. The visible appearance of the church's catholicity occurs at a time when nation-states appear ever weaker and when, in Samuel Huntington's phase, a clash of cultures grows ever more evident. The Catholic Church is one of the major transnational, transcultural actors on the world stage.

As the church in the United States becomes more American, the role of the priest as symbol and agent of Catholicity looms as especially important. While valuing the local church, he needs to remind Catholics that the church is wider than the parish, the diocese, and the United States; further, that the local church bears a measure of responsibility for churches elsewhere, especially those that are just beginning or are poor. Such stewardship is made concrete, for example, in the twinning of parishes with those in poor countries.

As the church becomes truly universal, there is a danger that a world church could become little more than a loose federation of national churches, a kind of British commonwealth of nations in which the fellowship of the Holy Spirit is reduced to a set of bureaucratic ties. The unity of the church must become a concern of all its catholic parts. It is a paramount duty of priests to remind themselves and their people that this wider church is always intimately present to every local church.

A universal point of view also makes it easier to identify the strengths and the weaknesses of American culture, especially those that may run counter to the Gospel like materialism, individualism, and neglect of the family.

Priest as Symbol and Agent of Apostolicity

The church is rooted in the faith of the apostles. Apostolic faith is a living tradition that each generation seeks to pass down intact to those who follow. In a world that changes every more swiftly, an old tradition is a repository of stabilizing wisdom. Apostolic faith gives both perspective and the wisdom of age, bringing a discerning eye to modern dilemmas. It helps to distinguish new human problems from perennial ones, to which faith gives the same reliable answer, phrased slightly differently in every generation.

Inevitably, the modern world has a tendency to view the wisdom of an old tradition as antiquated. The Catholic Church has learned to bear such reactions with patient equanimity, teaching the same truths with consistency and perseverance. Short-term skepticism often gives way to persistent effort. In this regard, the way the church has dealt with questions about the sanctity of life is exemplary. Slowly, the position of the church has come to look more persuasive and convincing.

The passing down of the tradition is never an impersonal affair, a matter of books and regulations. Teaching must come alive, for only a living tradition can be handed on. Priests have always played an active role in this transmission. But to play such a role effectively, priests themselves must be steeped in the apostolic faith, and that is no simple task. Rather, it is the fruit of a long education that has been internalized. But every preacher must eventually answer the question that St. Paul rightly poses to him: whose wisdom do you teach, that of the world or of Christ crucified? Only the latter gives life.

Priest as Memento

It is well to recall that priests as living symbols of Christ overlap all theological categories. They are too multifaceted and unpredictable to be contained or exhausted by theoretical considerations, regardless of their loftiness. On the contrary, living symbols often convey their essential messages in the commonplace, inconsequential gestures of ordinary life. Ministers of Christ, writes Cardinal Newman, are first a memento by the way they dress, the way they speak, their daily habits, and the way they fulfill their duties. In ordinary life, they are living reminders that life is short and God's judgment sure. On that basis alone, no age has fully embraced their presence.[13]

A priest who dresses in clerics these days can testify to the enduring truth of Newman's observations. A priest remains a potent symbol of duties toward God and neighbor that are often not met. If a priest is present, people generally do not swear or tell off-color stories, and if they do, they sometimes apologize. If an airplane hits bumpy weather, people may ask to go to confession. If they are dying, they ask for a priest. Such things happen suddenly and spontaneously with only a few preliminary words. For the same reason, the public failures of priests are carved in stone. Their failures could not be etched so deeply in public consciousness if priests had not loomed so large to begin with because of what they symbolize.

One way or another, by his presence, his dress, his general de-
meanor, a priest is a living memento of Christ's presence. There are
other such walking symbols, the poor, the hungry, and the naked
of Matthew 25. But in them, Christ is hidden. In the priest, he has
become publicly identifiable. This is both honor and burden, source
of praise and contumely, sometimes deserved, sometimes not.

Priests have often felt overcome by the priestly office and seldom felt themselves fully worthy of their calling. And, in point of
fact, they have not been ideally suited for the principal tasks of the
priesthood, preaching, sanctifying, and shepherding. The church in
its wisdom has never claimed that Christ chooses the brightest and
the best. Priests are not sure why they were called. A vocation at
heart remains a mystery. But God often calls the weak to make
them strong through his grace. Newman's final words to Christian
ministers have enduring merit. "Anyone who attempts to resist the
world, or to do other good things by his own strength, will be sure
to fall. We *can* do good things, but it is when God gives us the power
to do them."[14]

Priestly Spirituality

The chapter began with the person of Christ. It concludes with the
personality of priests in their weakness, their need for God's grace.
The asymmetry underscores a single point. The priesthood must be
understood at every point by the analogy of faith, the analogy from
above. If it is first and last the priesthood of Jesus Christ, Christ
must be the point of departure and arrival for all aspects of priestly
life. If the church is suffused and carried forward by the presence
of Christ, this must be true in a special way for priests. They are
weak, human vessels who endeavor to refract in their lives Christ's
presence in the church.

Therefore for seminarians: live up to the priesthood of Jesus
Christ to which you aspire. For priests: embody in your personal
life the priesthood of Jesus Christ that the church has entrusted
to you; endeavor to *become* in your personal life, what you *are*
by virtue of ordination. The terse wisdom on seminary walls in
the Latin of a bygone era, *Agnoscite quod agitis, Imitamini quod*

tractatis, is carried forward in the new rite of ordination at the presentation of the gifts in the words the bishop addresses to newly ordained priests: "Know what you are doing and imitate the mystery that you celebrate: model your life on the mystery of the Lord's cross."[15]

These words encapsulate the heroic response that the priesthood calls for, and they need to be emphasized at times when the fortunes of the priesthood are uncertain. This is what the church has done before in other difficult days, and this is what the church endeavors to do today. The truth is, the bar is now set higher for everyone. That is difficult news but good news, too. Priests are called to aspire to the highest ideals of their vocation and reflect those aspirations in their daily lives, so that the priesthood of Jesus Christ might shine forth clearly in their human efforts.

Chapter Ten

THE PRIEST AS MINISTER
OF THE WORD

~~~~~~~

ACCORDING TO VATICAN II, the three offices of Christ as prophet, priest, and shepherd are defining roles for the church as a whole that are given particular expression and active embodiment in the ministerial priesthood. The consequent way of describing the priesthood represents both a broadening of the tradition and, equally, a closer approximation to what priests actually do. They preach and teach, baptize and bless; they shepherd and counsel. These activities also constitute the path of holiness priests are asked to follow. This emphasis represented Vatican II's breakthrough. Heretofore, the classic model of priesthood of St. John Damascene regarded ministry as the outer expression of an inner font of priestly spirituality. Vatican II chose to reverse the directional flow: the exercise of priestly ministry is itself a major contributor to priestly holiness. Vatican II's Decree on the Ministry and Life of Priests acknowledges, "For it is through the sacred actions they perform every day, as through their whole ministry," that priests "are set on the right course to perfection of life."[1] These actions are not simply outward expressions of inner spirituality; they also affect the spirituality of priests in every way.

If the path to priestly holiness is through preaching, sanctifying, and shepherding, it carries a double challenge. The first regards the *interior attitudes* that priests bring to these tasks that both precede and follow the actual activity. They constitute the point of integration as the practice of ministry is transformed into personal spirituality. The second challenge looks to *practical skills.* Preaching, sanctifying, and shepherding are public duties requiring differing professional skills. These can be learned and honed, neglected or overlooked.

There may be a certain artificiality in examining these three roles separately. In point of fact, their strength is in their interplay. The priest who speaks at the parish council is the one who presides at the Eucharist. The one who munches a hot dog at the parish picnic and hears confessions on Saturday afternoon also signs the checks on Monday morning. An effort must be made not to slight the density of priestly ministry as these roles are examined individually. But we can examine each subject in more detail if the roles are looked at one at a time. And each has undergone its own particular development in the last decades.

ATTITUDES TOWARD
THE MINISTRY OF THE WORD

Catholics were often quite surprised that Vatican II had accorded the ministry of the word pride of place in priestly ministry. Should not the specifically priestly role as a witness to the centrality of the Eucharist in the Catholic tradition be given the honor? It can be argued that the council was simply following the order of learning that Vatican II speaks of, following St. Paul. "For since nobody can be saved who has not first believed, it is the first task of priests . . . to preach the Gospel of God to all men."[2]

But the larger truth may be that in a tradition in which the Bible played a secondary role for so long, a certain forgetfulness about the power of the word may have developed. That power was acknowledged anew by Vatican II. The word has its own unique and special capacity to make Christ present.

Listening and Speaking

"So Faith comes from what is heard, and what is heard comes through the word of Christ" (Rom. 10:17). Paradoxically, Paul's words seem to point to something that precedes human speech in all forms, namely, *listening*. This accords with the deepest logic of the Gospels. The disciples are those who hear the word of God and keep it. Mary first listens to the words the angel Gabriel speaks. It is really the interplay between listening and speech that is critical.

This is certainly the case with human speech. Animals may respond to complex signals, but this type of communication is a world apart from human discourse. Human speech resembles rather an ancient *discovery,* which Hellen Keller, for example, was able to replicate in her own experience. She understood that what her teacher was signing, w-a-t-e-r, pointed to the liquid flowing over hand. But her immediate fascination with words indicated that she quickly grasped their unique status.[3] They were far more than signals designating outside objects. Rather words corresponded to the inner world that reflective thought had carved into human consciousness. It is not too much to say that words were its first products and the gatekeeper to its domain. The deepest function of human speech is to reveal this inner world. Words unlock the inner depths of a person and give communicable shape to what was merely felt. Wasn't this finally the reason for Helen's joy? The discovery of words released her from her own inner world, as it simultaneously introduced her to a wider one. She could tell another her thoughts. She could listen to theirs. While words describe the world beyond us, their genius lies in their capacity to reveal and penetrate what is deep inside the human heart.

In the domain of language, writes Eugen Rosenstock-Heussy, the vocative and imperative mood, calls and commands, play a special role. They reveal human speech in its most primitive, dynamic form. People come to know themselves, he argues, only when they are called by name by another. So a child is told by its parents, "John, come here," "Mary, don't touch the stove." Only by means of the repeated calls and commands of others does self-consciousness grow in the individual. Only this way will Mary and John learn who they are in the first place. In the broadest sense, Rosenstock writes, "God has called me, therefore I am" represents a far more dependable human starting point than the Cartesian cogito. "I have been given my own name, therefore I am."[4] Names constitute a unique form of speech. They are very specific terms that seek to capture the uniqueness of an individual in a way that is socially communicable to others.

The Biblical Tradition

In the biblical tradition, calls and commands, vocatives and imperatives, play an essential role. It is not surprising that God chooses primal human speech as the special path through which revelation enters. God *calls* Moses, reveals His own *name* at the burning bush, and gives him a set of *commands* on Mount Sinai. The commandments call for reverence for the name as they forbid all images of this God; the name replaces the image as the key to worship. Israel can now worship a God whose name they know. In revealing his name, God has revealed part of himself, which brings the people of Israel into existence as a community. They exist because God called them. After the exile, the name becomes so powerful a symbol that its utterance with rare exception is forbidden.

Significantly, both Luke and Matthew begin the story of Jesus through a genealogy of names, of specific people in whom the seed of the messiah has rested. In Luke, as John the Baptist grows in the womb of his mother, his name incubates in the mouth of Zechariah who has been struck dumb. Jesus's name is given to Mary by the Angel Gabriel. Matthew quotes Isaiah 7:14, "They shall name him Emmanuel, which means 'God is with us' " (Matt. 1:23). In turn, Jesus calls the twelve by name and tells them to follow him. He doesn't tell them where they are going. He doesn't explain what tasks will be theirs. And he brooks no hesitation. He gives the simple command, "Come, follow me."

The heart of Jesus's preaching is the announcement that the kingdom of God is drawing near. God himself approaches. Jesus teaches his disciples to pray to the God of Israel, who bears a name too potent to utter, by calling him "Abba," a child's word for its father. The contrast could not be greater. Abba represents a deeper, more intimate penetration into God's name that becomes a self-definition of Jesus's followers: they call God Abba; they understand themselves as his children. Jesus teaches about the kingdom by his words and deeds, which resemble one another as complimentary forms of speech. His death becomes his own last word, giving his ministry the tight penetration of a single, deliberate word.

It is easy to understand why "Word" is applied to God to designate that interior part of his nature that he reveals to us. So John will write, "In the beginning was the Word, and the Word was with God, and the Word was God." "And the Word became flesh and lived among us" (John 1:1, 14). Once uttered, the Word took on a life of its own. The life, death, and resurrection of Jesus were a revelation of God's interior life, a parable of his love. And the message *about* Jesus is transmitted the same way the message *of* Jesus was delivered, by preaching. This preaching precedes and then carries the Gospels.

These thoughts underscore the power of the word in a tradition that is rediscovering its riches. That same power continues in the preaching of the church in our time. Jesus continues to call his followers by name. He asks them to follow him but he never tells them where they are going or what lies in store for them. Only the command, come and follow me.

This line of reasoning may seem to be uplifting to the believer but far removed from the realities of life. But this is not so. The power of the word is alive and well in today's world.

POPE JOHN PAUL II IN POLAND IN 1983 AND CUBA IN 1998

On Pope John Paul's second visit to Poland in 1983, he found his homeland under martial law, the Solidarity movement in disarray. A disheartened mood hung over the entire country. General Jaruzelski's right hand trembled as he read his greeting to the pope.[5] The general was right to be frightened. The effect of the pope's words on his demoralized Polish flock was electrifying. In his sermon at Czestochowa, he challenged his congregation to call good and evil by name. There was no mistaking what he meant. Then he softly said, writes George Weigel, "the unsayable word, solidarity"— solidarnosc—one of the few Polish words recognizable in English.[6] He was well on the way to broadening its meaning in all directions. In John Paul's preaching, it came to symbolize essential elements of the church's social teaching, a new consciousness, a way of life.[7]

John Paul not only reinvigorated the mood of his homeland. The word of God in his mouth effectively stripped the Communist government of moral authority. Calling good and evil by name meant separating power from authority. The government may have retained coercive power, but John Paul II spoke with authority and people listened to him. They still feared government power but the voice of the government grew weaker and weaker as its authority died.

He began to do the same thing in Cuba in 1998. On January 25 in the Plaza of the Revolution, his preaching caught fire under the competing icons of Che Guevara at one end of the plaza and a ten-story-tall picture of the Sacred Heart at the other. Although government officials greeted him on arrival, no one was smiling at the end of his homily when the crowd began to chant, "The pope is free and wants us all to be free."[8]

There are lessons in the example of John Paul II in Poland and Cuba for seminarians and priests to ponder as they form their own interior attitudes about preaching.

First, the power of the word. The power of the word lies in its ability to rightly identify people and situations. John Paul's challenge to name good and evil and the first mention of the forbidden word "solidarity" were momentous displays of word-power. Right names unlock other words. John Paul gave his Polish flock words for their hopes and aspirations in 1983. They literally lifted themselves up by his words and made his words their own. They then came roaring back to him with their contribution added. The interchange contains an enduring lesson. A good preacher gives his congregation a set of words for their feelings, for their hopes and aspirations, for their fears and misgivings. If they strike home, his words become theirs.

Second, the independence of words. This was especially evident in Cuba. Often the pope's words came out sluggishly. But no matter what the difficulty for him in saying them, once out there, they at once took on a life of their own, often landing like bomb shells. Words, once spoken, have their own independence.

Third, the timing of words. The Scriptures say that Jesus was born in the fullness of time. This too applies to every preached word. When is it the right time to preach, when to remain silent? Clearly 1979 was too early for much of John Paul's preaching in Poland. But in 1987 it would have been too late. Every preacher must weigh the same question. Is the time ripe for this word? Is this the time for a word of confrontation or a word of consolation, a hard word or an encouraging one? It is well to weigh the timing of words in advance because, once spoken, they cannot be taken back. A hard word to a congregation at the wrong moment can become a serious public mistake.

Fourth, listening to words. People truly listen only to those who speak with authority, as we saw in Poland and Cuba. A congregation has inalienable discretionary authority. It can choose to listen or not. There is no worse fate for the spoken word than to fall on deaf ears or, even worse, on ears deliberately closed.

One listens and takes in words on one end, then speaks on the other. What counts is what happens in between. The preacher's interior attitudes are a complex mechanism for processing, digesting, and finally shaping into an intelligible message for others what he himself has heard. He is shaping words through which others can understand and digest their own experience and then speak themselves.

Two points about reading and prayer. A congregation is aware whether the preacher is a reader and how widely he reads. This is the difference between fresh preaching and stale homilies, between the same old message repeated again and again and something new. Reading may not be the only way to learn, but it is surely the most reliable way to gain complex new ideas and a good way to keep preaching fresh and lively. The only thing more evident is whether a preacher has prayed about and pondered what he is saying. Out of which level or depth of personality do these words come? How much personal authority do they carry? Since a congregation listens only to someone who speaks with authority, the preacher must also take himself seriously. If he does not, he will speak carelessly, without deliberation, and off the cuff on serious matters. Only a person who takes himself seriously believes his words can make a difference.

If Christ's spirit prays in the human heart, surely that same spirit seeks to speak through the words of a preacher. This is how Jesus's message came to his followers and how it is handed on. But by the same token, God's spirit requires the best a preacher has to offer. This is the ultimate reason he listens closely, prepares carefully, reads and prays himself: to make his human words into fitting instruments for God's word.

THE PRACTICE OF THE MINISTRY
OF THE WORD

The ministry of the word speaks with three distinct voices. Sometimes the words "prophet," "teacher," and "preacher" are used interchangeably. In reality, they are all different. The three together remind us of the breadth of the word, the diverse ways in which it has appeared, and the different ways in which it is proclaimed. All three have differing relevance to the ministry of the word that priests exercise.

Prophet

Prophecy is the rarest voice. The Old Testament reminds us that there are schools only for false prophets, not true ones. The true prophetic call descends on the individual vertically and inexplicably. No instruction manual accompanies it. Priests in our tradition are institutional figures who belong to a worldwide order of priests. They are not the usual recipients of such a call. Experience also teaches that claimants to extraordinary gifts deserve close scrutiny. A noted biblical scholar once wryly observed that in all Israel only a handful of prophets appeared, a fact that gave him pause in the late 1960s when divinity schools seemed regularly to graduate twenty to thirty prophets a year. Yet if the prophetic charism is rare, it is also an enduring form of the Word, which appears when and where it chooses.

In recent years, some Catholic priests and bishops have been impelled to act in a prophetic way to be faithful to their duties as shepherds. Bishop Robert Bello in East Timor and Archbishop Oscar Romero in El Salvador are but two of those who, in the name of human rights, have felt compelled to raise a prophetic voice. A witness to their authenticity is that they did not choose to become prophets. Rather, the role was thrust on them. It is not surprising that large institutions are seldom entirely comfortable with a prophet in their midst. Who is?

The more common translation of the prophetic challenge for priests is that they be persons of character who act with integrity. From time to time, they may find it necessary to speak out publicly on injustice in society and wrong policies in government. Such preaching is effective only if one's personal life is marked by integrity.

Though the prophetic voice remains, it does not describe the usual challenges of the ministry of the word that confront priests. In practical terms, teaching and preaching are the more typical ones.

Teacher

Timing is always crucial in the ministry of the word, and this is especially the case in regard to teaching at the present moment. Almost two generations after a major council, one might say the time is ripe for the role of priest as teacher. While Vatican II understood itself as a pastoral council that undertook an updating, not a major revision of Catholic doctrine, the *style* that the council adopted contrasted so sharply with older forms of church teaching that an inevitable period of disorientation followed. Catholics were no longer able to discriminate between essential and incidental changes, and very little was explained in advance. By the by, they learned, for example, that limbo had been "phased out," a hard blow to generations whose pennies, dimes, and dollars had ransomed countless pagan babies. What about all those babies who died with the stain of original sin on their soul? Where were they now? Or was original sin also in trouble? And how about purgatory? Was it closed for repairs or had it been phased out? At the very least, purgatory now seemed under new management. Certainly, Catholics no longer prayed with such frequency or fervor for the "poor souls in purgatory," a phrase that seems to belong to an

older era. Apparently most people were now whisked directly from
their earthly dwelling place to a new home in the kingdom with
no intermediate stops. And then Catholics learned that although
Hell existed, it was unlikely that anyone was there. That seemed
odd. How about Adolf Hitler and Joseph Stalin and all the other
heinous characters in which the twentieth century seemed to spe-
cialize? Were they also given a pass or placed in a special annex,
perhaps . . . in limbo?

All of this describes not a change of doctrine but of *sensibility.*
The new atmosphere the council introduced, however, *was* different. The first generation of catechetical texts after Vatican II
struggled with the changes in a predictable way. They dissolved
Catholicism, by any measure a doctrinal religion, into a set of pas-
tel attitudes — love of God, love of neighbor, patience with self,
toleration of others. Such truths were often just the right size for
classroom banners. Thus "collage" Catholicism was born, leaving
in its wake a generation of Catholics with doctrinal amnesia. Only
as adults did they come to recognize, often with chagrin, that Catholicism has a long, articulate doctrinal tradition with hard, thorny
edges that Vatican II, despite the change in sensibility, meant to
hand on intact.

The appearance of the *Catechism of the Catholic Church (1992)*
was a sign of the times and an eye-opener. While some greeted it
with mild disdain, the *Catechism* — a compendium of Catholic
teaching on doctrine, sacraments, morality, and prayer — quickly
became a runaway best seller. It came as a surprise and perhaps a
relief to some Catholics that the church could still produce a catechism. But the real truth about its success was that the *Catechism*
addressed a felt need with which almost all Catholics could identify. How could a generation with scant acquaintance with the faith
pass on that same faith to their children without a fixed point of
reference? Here the real function of the *Catechism* comes to light.
It was meant to act as a master catechism from which a generation
of more accessible, popular texts might be prepared. The bishops
wisely established the *Office for the Catechism* to oversee this first
generation of texts, attesting to their conformity with the original.

The past ten years has witnessed a steady improvement of catechetical texts as well as greater surety by the bishops in overseeing and encouraging their development.

The problem facing newly ordained priests may be that they continue to have only limited familiarity with the *Catechism.* Indeed, teachers and students may well be more acquainted with the text than the local priest. If there is a clearly identifiable challenge facing newly ordained priests as teachers, it is right here: first-hand familiarity with the *Catechism.* Whatever its shortcomings, its stature will only grow with time. Such is the fate of major catechisms. The present one will play a central role on all levels of teaching in the church in the future.

But the overriding challenge to priests and people alike is broader still. How do we pass on the faith to our children with integrity? The new *Catechism* may serve to revive an older Catholic tradition, a teaching pattern really, that has served the church well over the centuries. The faith is first learned, memorized, in simple formulas whose meaning children barely grasp. Then the same material is circled many times in subsequent years. Intelligible layers of meaning are added with each turn. Gradually, a doctrinal sensibility, a *feel,* begins to emerge that can discriminate between essentials and accidentals, mystery from obfuscation. Speculative questions arise at the proper moment. The end product is the distinctive consciousness that is an abiding characteristic of the classic Catholic mind-set, a person firmly grounded in the faith who can acknowledge its bewildering nuance and inexhaustible mystery. While the madman lives in a "clean and well-lit prison of one idea," Chesterton writes, true answers call for a key and a lock, both of which are complicated.[9] Such is our faith. Passing down a complex tradition is no mean feat. At the very least, it calls for a game plan devised well in advance.

Familiarity with the *Catechism* hardly exhausts the challenges facing priests as teachers. They must also stay abreast of theology, a challenges that bristles with its own difficulties. With fewer and fewer priests absorbed with more and more pastoral duties, it is a major logistical problem to find quiet time for concentrated reading. And what to read? Scholarly journals, without prejudice to their contribution, can hardly be described as scintillating reading for the busy priest — a fact perhaps illustrative of the larger theological scene at the moment. The number of theologians named cardinals in recent years — Yves Congar, Aloys Grillmeier, Avery Dulles, Walter Kasper, and Karl Lehman — is a reminder of theology's success at Vatican II, which the church is still digesting and absorbing. After a generation of such fecundity it is not surprising that theology may find itself in a recuperative moment. This may also be the time to revisit the great twentieth-century theologians who graced the last century. Classic thinkers like Newman, Moehler, and Pascal are perennially relevant.

Whatever the choice of serious reading, old advice is still the best: if you want to learn something yourself, then teach it to others. Adult education has always been a dependable forum for priests to keep up on their own reading, rendering personal study more focused and directed. But whatever the method, concentrated study is the only sure way to gain new ideas for preaching and teaching. On the information highway, where everything moves with increasing speed, in theology, sadly, only a single-lane road leads into town.

Preacher

The ministry of the word stretches across vast territory. It may mean a word of praise or consolation, at times a word of rebuke, other times, a challenge to reform. It may also take the simple form of teaching a tradition, as it is passed from one generation to the next. Preaching draws these strands together, varying the mix for the occasion. The preached word is guided by two pole stars: the written word of God on the one hand and the varying needs of the congregation on the other. The homily in particular is a reflection on the word of God, proclaimed in the liturgical assembly, addressed to the gathered Christian faithful. It occupies the heart and center of the ministry of the word.

Such concepts are relatively new to Catholics. In establishing the practical challenge of preaching, it is helpful to understand how the biblical word and the task of preaching have evolved in the Catholic tradition in the past two generations. Against this background, the varying expectations of Catholics in the pews can be understood as well as the strengths and weaknesses of Catholic preachers as they seek to rekindle the legacy of the word of God.

The great magna charta of Catholic biblical studies, *Divino Afflante Spiritu* (1943), appeared barely one generation before Vatican II. The first pitched battles of the council were fought about the topic of revelation and a great part of the debate pertained to *Divino Afflante Spiritu*. Does the church continue along the critical path the encyclical had opened? In particular, does it place the Scripture in its historical setting to discern the literal sense of the biblical text? The Dogmatic Constitution on Revelation, *Dei Verbum*, became in the end a ringing endorsement of the 1943 encyclical, extending the historical critical approach to the interpretation of the Gospels.

Catholics, however, are still in the process of digesting this enormous rediscovery of the word of God. The plain fact is that for centuries after the Reformation, it was as if the Christian inheritance of word and sacrament had been divided. Catholics kept the sacraments, Protestants, the word of God. Now, happily, the rediscovery of the word of God has become a common bond that unites Catholics with other Christians, particularly the churches of the Reformation.

But the path was not always easy for Catholic congregations or their preachers in the first generation after Vatican II. Both began with low expectations. What was delivered from the pulpit before the council was called a "sermon," sometimes following a teaching outline distributed by the diocese that had little to do with the Sunday Scriptures. It seemed almost an optional part of Sunday mass that few took seriously. Daily preaching was unheard of. So when Catholics received the gift of the word after Vatican II, no one was quite sure how to open the package or what to do with the gift when it was unwrapped. Preaching was off to an uneven start. Older priests were often unschooled in modern biblical exegesis and simply became more unsure of themselves. Younger priests often delivered too much historical exegesis, more sure of what the text meant two millennia ago than of its relevance to the congregation in front of them. Moreover, the desire to *pray* the Bible puzzled almost everyone.

So as the word of God was praised in official documents and Bibles were adorned and enthroned in an honored place in public, a lack of inner balance was everywhere evident and most prominently displayed in the preacher himself. The priest, for so long a silent figure at the liturgy, now became a man of many words. Sunday homilies were often long and rambling. Daily preaching, an art of great discretion, became instead the favored venue for woolly thoughts, the on-switch flipped as internal ruminations were broadcast to the general public. If there was a common fault, it was logorrhea. Too many words. In short, the shift from relative neglect of the word of God to a position of major importance in the Catholic tradition was going to take time. The move from sermon to homily was not so simple.

The problem is twofold. There is the usual difficulty of biblical preaching in Christian churches: how to make an ancient text relevant to the contemporary scene. The specifically Catholic challenge is to find the right place for the homily in the overall structure of the eucharistic celebration. The homily is part of the celebration of the word, but even more it is a joint celebration of word and sacrament. Time is the easiest measure. If the Sunday Eucharist runs about an hour or more, how long should the homily be? Ultimately the liturgy of the word and the homily should fit together in the celebration of the sacrament and the two parts of the Eucharist should be roughly symmetrical.

With the challenge of preaching now in its second generation, new issues have emerged. The historical-critical method has been joined by other methods of literary analysis, including rhetorical, narrative, and semiotic. The critical task has become more complex and diffuse. An attractive alternative these days is to bypass such complexity in favor of a "spiritual interpretation," which often means a fundamentalist reading of the biblical text. *The Interpretation of the Bible in the Church* of the Pontifical Biblical Commission (1992) admirably describes the current situation, delivering as well a withering commentary on biblical fundamentalism. The Catholic commitment to a critical approach could not be more plainly stated.[10]

Seminaries and schools of theology have taken the challenge of preaching seriously and made steady improvement in the teaching of homiletics. There are, though, intractable problems that do not yield easily to any solution. The biggest is the simple but undeniable fact that some seminarians grasp from the start how to preach while others seem permanently impaired. Preaching is like riding a bicycle. After a few tries, some get the hang of it and find their balance. For others, the venture is forever precarious. What is especially difficult is that priestly aptitudes for preaching often are set for life at ordination. Practice does not make perfect; it only begets more of the same.

CATHOLIC EXPECTATIONS

In the town of Beaver Falls, Pennsylvania, a middle-aged steel worker heard a young priest at mass announce that he taught homiletics at a seminary and was interested in hearing what Catholics thought about preaching. The man approached the priest after mass. "Say," he asked, "does that mean you teach seminarians how to preach?"

"Yes," replied the priest.

"Well," said the man, "you tell your students this. Each day when I go to work my wife packs two sandwiches for me in my lunch pail. When I open it, there they are, two sandwiches. I can count on it. When I go to mass on Sunday, what I want are two thoughts that will last me until Wednesday, two things I can think about as I drive back and forth to work or when I have time to myself. Two thoughts till Wednesday. I can make it through the rest of the week on my own. What's the difference between good and bad preaching? Easy answer. My wife is homebound. She always asks me after mass, 'What did the priest say?' When it's a good homily, I can repeat what the priest said in one or two sentences. When I can't do that, it's a bad homily."

INEFFECTIVE PREACHING

Father extracted one or two thoughts from the Gospel. Last week's line was, "life is always a surprise." Then he would repeat it again

*and again. If there was any freshness to the thought, it was like beef
jerky by the time he got done with it. No surprises left. But we could
take that. It was the endings that got us. He never knew how to end
a homily. He would circle the field again and again like a Piper Cub
looking for a landing strip. But he never landed. We thought, "This
is going to be it, the end of the homily." The wheels have almost
touched down. But then he pulled back on the stick and circled
the field again. Another thought. This could go on five or six times.
"Land the darn thing," one man muttered to his wife. People often
felt a bit queasy when he finally managed to end his homily.*

EFFECTIVE PREACHING

*The priest took two or three thoughts from the readings for people to
ponder. He had carefully formulated how to phrase these thoughts.
He put them in a way you could easily remember. He never repeated himself. He said each one once, said it clearly, and usually
illustrated the thoughts with a story. The stories were wonderful.
Then he stopped and sat down. He seldom talked more than eight
or nine minutes. The steel worker liked to go to this mass because
he could repeat to his wife exactly what the priest said.*

*Though he never repeated himself, the priest repeated some hom-
ilies whole and entire every year. He told people he was going to
do it. He gave the same homily for Ash Wednesday and All Saints
Day. People liked it. He often quoted Dr. Johnson that people were
less in need of instruction than of helpful reminders. That is what
he gave them. He also repeated stories he liked. People looked forward to it. His best ones they knew by heart. Sometimes he asked
a parishioner to deliver the punch line. Everyone laughed.*

*When he sat down, people often thought, "I wish he would have
gone on a little longer." Someone told him this and he smiled.*

*"What a nice thing to say. I hope that makes you want to come
back next week." It did.*

In conclusion, three rules for no-fault preaching. They are not
simple or sophisticated; they are both. Rule One: *Have something*

to say. Be able to write down in two sentences what the homily is about. Two clear, simple sentences. Rule Two: *Say it once.* The common mistake of preachers is to think that repetition strengthens a point. Skilled alliteration may. But repetition usually weakens it. It muddies the message, conveying the impression that the homilist is thinking out loud, trying to decide what he wants to say. Probably often the case. Far better to work out a concise phrasing and say it once, which is also far easier to remember than a complex thought that unravels with each repetition. Stories always help. Rule Three: *Stop!* How many homilies have been improved by lengthening them? How many homilies would have been improved if the preacher had stopped halfway through? "It is true that the Spirit opens the heart," writes Käsemann, "but sometimes it also stops the mouth."[11]

Chapter Eleven

THE PRIEST AS MINISTER
OF THE SACRAMENT

~~~~~~~~~

T HE SECOND OFFICE of Christ as priest stands at the heart and
center of the traditional Catholic understanding of the priesthood. Yet even the heart and center were transformed at Vatican II.
This chapter explores that special transformation.

The starting point is the traditional Latin phrase *ex opere operato* (literally, by the work worked), which encapsulates centuries
of vexing history dating back to the Donatist controversy in the
fourth and fifth centuries, centering on very practical questions. Are
the sacraments performed by an unworthy priest, say, an apostate
priest, valid? Are they true sacraments? The Latin phrase appears
among theologians as early as the thirteenth century. It is incorpo-
rated into the canons of the Council of Trent in its seventh session
in 1547 in the general discussion of sacraments.[1]

What arose from practical controversy and passed into a tech-
nical distinction enshrines a theological statement of the highest
order. Christ is the author of the sacraments. It is Christ who bap-
tizes, Christ who confirms. Acting through the priest, it is Christ
who changes bread and wine into the Body and Blood of Christ.
Since Christ is their author, the validity of the sacraments does
not depend on the worthiness or the holiness of the minister. Or
even his faith. The priest's essential contribution is a right intention. He intends to do what the church intends. It is the faith of
the church that carries the human contribution to the validity of
the sacraments. The complementary Latin phrase *ex opere operantis* refers to the subjective contribution of the minister, a laudatory
but secondary addition, not necessary for valid or licit sacraments.

This seemingly abstract discussion became as critical a bone of
contention at the Reformation as the doctrine of justification. It

certainly marked the line of demarcation in worship between the churches of the Reformation and Roman Catholicism; the less significant the sacramental life of a particular church, the larger the difference loomed. At the center was Christ's presence in the Eucharist; is it a real or symbolic one? By extension, was Christ truly present in the other sacraments?

The insistence on the objective character of the sacraments with Christ as their author had a large impact on the Catholic Church itself. It stood at every point behind the Council of Trent's teaching on the sacraments and the mass of Pius V of 1570, a reform of the Eucharist that stood largely unchanged for four hundred years until replaced by the mass of Paul VI of 1970. It was nothing less than a central pillar of Catholic worship from the Reformation until the middle of the twentieth century.

Significantly in the mass of Pius V, the rubrics regulated each and every gesture of the priest, and priests were obliged to follow them under pain of sin. The result was that the personality of the celebrant was virtually expunged from the Eucharist, reduced to a human cipher, so that the role of Christ, author of the Eucharist, could shine forth more clearly. It would be difficult for formal principles to find better practical expression than in the ways in which *ex opere operato* and *ex opere operantis* were woven into the fabric of the mass of 1570. The principles became practice and, just as quickly, spirituality.

That, of course, is the point. This assemblage of gestures generated a *religious sensibility* that deeply affected priests and people in every way, creating a special climate in which Catholic devotional piety outside the mass could flourish. The priest was described as "saying" or "reading" mass, depending on the language. (Rarely was it said that he "prayed" the mass. His personal prayers often preceded the mass. It was more common after mass for the priest to make a personal thanksgiving. But these prayers were not to be confused with the official prayers of the eucharistic sacrifice.) "Reverently" saying mass meant that he avoided any hint of theatricality or personalization, that he followed the rubrics in a considered way. Priests did not have "styles" when they said mass. They may have developed "idiosyncrasies," personal quirks, but only those who attended mass regularly noticed them. It was a wonderful thing, Catholics said, to be able to attend the same mass in Calcutta, Berlin, and New York. More than one Catholic extolled the wisdom of the church in reducing the personality of the priest to a shadow presence that cannot annoy and usually does not distract. All signals to the priest, direct and indirect, told him the mass should not be personalized. Christ is the author, the priest an interchangeable cog in the great sacrifice of the mass, the unbloody repetition of Christ's saving death on Calvary.

The Catholic faithful were also reduced to a shadowy presence. They "attended" mass, although it became more and more common for people to follow the words of the priest in their missals. But they regarded themselves as observers or spectators who watched the priest say mass in front of them. It was not uncommon for people to pray the rosary during mass. It is not difficult to understand why a flourishing devotional life sprang up outside the mass in which normal human feelings, desires, and wishes could be expressed more adequately. The devotional life of the church was a subjective outlet that the objective character of the mass encouraged. Likewise, no one asked if people "got anything out" of the mass or if they "enjoyed" the mass. Priests and people would have treated such a question with disdain, if not contempt. It was a privilege to be present.

The infinite merits of a single mass were not reckoned in terms of euphoric human feelings, fleeting as they inevitably were. The mass contained untold rewards for eternal life, benefits for the poor souls in purgatory and perhaps for one's own soul when counted one day among their number. A character of Iris Murdoch's caught the ethos and the austere attraction of the old liturgy when he mused, "The Mass remained, not consoling, not uplifting but in some way factual. It contained for him no assurance that all would be made well that was not well. It simply existed as a kind of pure reality separate from the weaving of his own thoughts."[2]

A great modern reform movement, stretching back into the nineteenth century, centered on liturgical renewal. This movement was given official encouragement, and the dialogue mass in Latin, for example, had become a regular form of eucharistic celebration in the twentieth century. Liturgical renewal was addressed at the highest level of church life in Pius XII's 1948 encyclical *Mediator Dei.* The revised liturgy for Holy Week of 1955 represented another significant milestone. Yet not even the most fervent advocate of renewal could have envisioned how fully Vatican II would embrace the challenge of liturgical reform. Authors describe the inviting style of the documents of Vatican II, and the description is largely apt. But in the latter chapters of the Constitution on the Liturgy, the velvet glove was removed, revealing a steely, forceful hand that mandated sweeping liturgical reforms. The leading principle was boldly proclaimed in paragraph 14 of the Constitution on the Liturgy. The "aim" of the reform "to be considered before all else" is the "full, conscious, active participation of all the faithful." The document immediately enjoined all pastors to implement the principle and ordered that seminary liturgical training be adapted accordingly. The Constitution on the Liturgy meant business.

This principle is coupled with another from *Lumen Gentium* that the priest in the person of Christ effects the eucharistic sacrifice and offers it to God in the name of the whole people of God, that is, in the name of the church. This was an ancient but a novel accent too, essential to the priestly role in every way. Robert Sokolowski carefully traces the Christological and ecclesiological moments of the canon.[3] The Words of Institution are phrased in the first person singular, "This is my Body." Here the great Christological moment occurs. But the prayers leading up to and following the words of institution begin characteristically in the plural "We, your people and your ministers." The eucharistic prayer is offered by the assembled faithful with the priest as their spokesperson.

When these elements are brought together, the effect is revolutionary. The aim of "full, conscious, active participation" is applied to the faithful, but it applied in equal measure to the priest. This marked a decisive turn in the priestly role. The cipher-like presence of the priest at the mass of Pius V can hardly be described as a form of "full, conscious, active" participation. It was quite the opposite; the living priestly presence had previously been deliberately expunged. Therefore the first and decisive principle of the reform revolutionized the role of priest and people alike. In doing so, it joined the priest and the worshiping assembly all the more closely together. The priest was not simply a Christological simulacrum. He was a leader of prayer for the Christian community, gathered together to offer the great eucharistic sacrifice.

Many of these sentiments were found in *Mediator Dei*, but the genius of Vatican II was to combine them with two practical gestures. The first was the introduction of the vernacular language; the second was the simple act of turning around the altar. This was a giant step, creating a new sensibility for priest and people alike. The traditional Catholic practice of saying mass facing East was now characterized as "mass facing the wall," its very description a form of disparagement. By contrast, "mass facing the people" was the nobler way, the path better angels were asking Catholics to follow.

The two gestures — the vernacular language and mass facing the people — dovetailed exactly, and an interactive dynamic was formally established. Something began to emerge for which no one was prepared. An electric spark arced across separate points. New roles for priests and people came to life.

The resistance to turning around the altars remains a distant but vivid reminder of the vast sea change that was underway. Such memories now have the status of long-forgotten dinosaur bones, but they deserve a brief resurrection here to illumine the difference a single gesture made and the difficulty it posed for some priests.

MASS FACING THE PEOPLE IN 1964 AND 1967

Naturally the rector would turn the altar around as he was instructed to do. He taught the seminarians that obedience that really counted came when you were asked to do something you did not want to do. Now he had to do that himself. He had a flimsy portable altar constructed. He placed it in front of a vast marble altar, covered by a baldachin supported by four massive chocolate marble pillars. The portable altar was like a wooden raft adrift in a sea of marble. Further, he had a large crucifix and even larger "altar cards" placed at the front of the portable altar. (This was the way old mass was set up with repeated prayers and readings on large cards at the front of the altar.) You could barely see him behind the cards. One wit dubbed it "mass facing the Altar Cards."

Three years later, when mass was in English, Father Richard Finster still felt uncomfortable. He felt that people were staring at him when he said mass. And so they were. But he didn't care for it one bit. He felt affronted and confused. He felt that people wanted something from him. He wasn't sure what it was or how to give it. Worse, he felt what he did have to offer was no longer needed.

When the new mass of Paul VI emerged in 1970, it was clear that a paradigm shift had taken place, radically and irrevocably reshaping the roles of both priest and people. The priest was the head of a worshiping community, the leader of the band. His own personal activity mirrored and encouraged that "full, active, conscious participation" of the community that the Constitution on the Liturgy had mandated.

These changes reflected vast seismic shifts in Catholic worship that will take many generations to absorb. As the mass of Pius V slipped irretrievably below the surface, not only a new mass but a new *religious sensibility* emerged, a new *feel* to Catholic worship. Like in other changes, it was both evolutionary and revolutionary. While the principle of *ex opere operato* still undergirded the sacraments — Christ is their author — its pale counterpart, *ex opere operantis*, now appeared in considerably brighter plumage. The personality of the priest stepped to the fore. The rubrics of the new mass encouraged the shift: first, there were fewer of them and the role of the priest was no longer so closely choreographed; second, and even more amazing, he was permitted to improvise. The rubrics enjoined him, for example, to introduce a prayer "in these or similar words." This was an unheard of step at mass!

INTERIOR ATTITUDES

The three offices of Christ as prophet, priest, and shepherd comprise a set of *interior attitudes* and *practical skills* as they apply to priests. Nowhere was the dramatic change in the priesthood more graphically displayed than in the shift of interior attitudes toward this second office. In regard to priest as prophet or shepherd, the interior change came by way of *enlargement*. New attitudes were required. In regard to the core of the priestly role, though, the change came by way of *replacement*. An old mind-set had to go; a new one had to take its place, by any measure a more difficult path. And there was no middle ground, no bridge to get from one side to the other.

The older mind-set has appeared more than once as the person of Father Richard Finster was introduced to exemplify it. His priestly role model was the classic one of St. John Damascene, self-contained monk-priest. This ideal was etched into a priest's personality by twelve years of relentless seminary formation. It produced priests with deeply private personal piety who avoided displays of external devotion. Even more broadly, they seemed to avoid all displays of emotion. They said mass every day reverently and correctly and took pride in it. They said their private prayers. Their personal distance from gestures of public worship was in its own way an act of devotion, of devout restraint.

What the new liturgy asked of such priests was entirely novel. It asked that their personal prayer now be inserted into official, public worship, into the mass now called the "Eucharist." Surprisingly, many priests made this large transition remarkably well. All were buoyed by the popularity of the new liturgy. But some also found that their old instincts were no longer dependable. Their natural steering mechanism faltered. They were like older residents of the former Soviet Union or East Germany who could not make their way in the new nation, senior citizens pondering the mysteries of the latest version of Windows, lost souls in a new world.

This meant that after the council, the transition to a new generation of priest occurred all too abruptly. Certainly there were fights about removing the altar rail and moving the tabernacle, but essentially the battles were over quickly. The older generation found it easier simply to cede the field. They took early retirement and succumbed in higher numbers to strokes and heart attacks. The more thoughtful of their number realized that they had been left behind when the tide turned.

The field was clear for the *new breed*. The best of them came from the tail end of the Catholic immigrant culture before it merged into the American mainstream. This generation of priests was ordained with a clear mandate. They were to implement the changes of Vatican II; they were to be the foot soldiers of the reforms on the front line. Here was a new mind-set. They understood not only the letter but the ethos of the council and reveled in the new era that was dawning. It resembled at times a Catholic version of the age of Aquarius.

FATHER PAT'S MASS

Over the speaker in the dining room, Father Finster could hear Father Pat's mass, the eleven o'clock. Personally, he didn't like to say this mass. Too crowded. And the people always seemed distracted. After the sign of the cross, Pat began, "The Lord be with You."

The standard response came back, "And also with you."

"Thank you," said the young priest.

The older man was stunned. " 'THANK YOU?' 'Thank you' was not a liturgical response!" he muttered to himself.

"Morning, folks," said Father Pat.

"Morning, Father Pat," they roared.

"Ready for the Steeler game this afternoon?" Another roar. "But now the Eucharist. Let us pause for a moment."

The packed church became instantly silent. Father Finster was amazed. The young priest was . . . interacting with the congregation. Much more than that. With his soft voice and laconic style, he was the master of the situation. But the dismissal rite was what really got him. Not the standard, "The mass is ended. Go in peace." No. "The mass is NEVER ended! Go forth to live the Eucharist." Then a pause. "And Go, Steelers!"

The congregation roared back, "Thanks be to God!"

"Go, Steelers!"

"Go, Pat!"

Father Pat's mass illustrates general characteristics of the new situation and the larger trajectory they established over time. First, the defining characteristic of this new generation of priests was the way they celebrated the liturgy. They knew the mass was a communal celebration. The habit of "private masses" virtually disappeared overnight. They also knew they were called to *pray*, not *say* the mass. They understood themselves as active leaders of prayer in active worshiping communities.

Second, they were not fearful of the newfound freedom. On the contrary, they reveled in it. If the new rubrics offered some liberties, they often took more. Prayers were dropped, genuflections omitted, the Eucharistic Prayer altered. A casual personal style — light humor, football scores, personal revelations — describes the usual mix. One observer put it this way: it was as if in a ten-year period, the Catholic mass went from stylized Kabuki theater to a late night talk show with the priest as the genial host.

Third, if history moves like a pendulum, it was almost inevitable that this first generation would overly personalize the new liturgy, taking too many liberties. But the situation also seemed to contain a built-in corrective. Too much improvisation quickly became irksome. It didn't wear well when every mass was a surprise. Ritual demands predictability. Both priests and people need to know what to expect. The younger generation of priests seems little inclined to continue the improvising proclivities of the first generation of priest-liturgist. Inevitably, a change of generation will complete the initial shakedown cruise of the new liturgy.

Fourth, as preaching and styles of presiding merged, they underscored a major downside of the new liturgy. It left priests far too exposed. It revealed too much about them personally. Just as the old liturgy hid priests's personalities behind a wall of rubrics, the new liturgy revealed their personality at every turn. The first years after the council were replete with sad episodes of far too personal, self-revealing homilies, pleas for sympathy from the congregation that elicited pity, then mild contempt.

Thoughtful priests moved to limit exposure. It has become more common for priests to "follow the book," weighing more carefully their ad libs. If they could not see the dangers in themselves, they surely saw it in others. While the standard prayers may leave something to be desired, they usually surpass the free-form orisons of others. The new liturgy is to be *moderately* personalized. But moderation was a hard-fought quantum that did not come easily or quickly.

It is clear now, how much this new generation of priests was inundated with new freedoms: in the liturgy, in moral theology, in social roles. And as new freedoms opened, old constraints fell away. Newfound freedoms elsewhere quickly found their way to the arena of sexuality like steel filings drawn to a magnet. For those who entered the seminary at twelve or thirteen, the attraction seemed at times irresistible.

PRACTICAL SKILLS

It would have made little sense to speak of "skill" in regard to the old liturgy. There was often a practicum in the final year of theology in which priests were instructed on how to say a correct mass. They usually had to pass a "mass exam" to demonstrate their mastery of the technique. Over the years, they may have developed idiosyncrasies. But there was only one mass no matter who said it. The new liturgy forced the acknowledgment of slightly differing *styles of celebration* as an objective component of Catholic worship. Every seminary and theological center offers at least one course in celebration for priest candidates. Many of the same techniques as in homiletics are used, e.g., videotaping. In many ways, styles of preaching and of celebration are closely connected in Catholic worship, conforming to the nature of the eucharistic celebration. But while much more time is devoted to preaching before ordination, celebration is usually limited to a single course. This means that while styles of celebration may have become an important, objective component of Catholic worship, they are largely learned after ordination. The art of celebration is left, in the last analysis, to the world of practice, left to be picked up along the way catch as catch can. This is called learning in the school of hard knocks. In the school of hard knocks, it is said, people never know when they pass, only when they flunk, but that news comes swiftly. Wisdom only follows slowly and with a fair dose of pain. What is offered here are some thoughts to ponder and a few rules of thumb.

Personal Presence

The liturgy needs to be moderately personalized. It is difficult for seminarians preparing for the priesthood to appreciate fully how much the liturgy, homily, and style of celebration together reveal about a priest personally without his intending or realizing it.

The priest should be very cautious about personal revelations. A little bit goes a long way. A congregation that has heard a man preach for six months and watched the way he presides at the Eucharist becomes intimately acquainted with the contours of his heart. If every homily is first preached to the preacher himself, the congregation is privy to the best of a priest's interior dialogue with God. All of this happens inevitably and naturally. If a priest consciously decides to make further personal revelations, he must realize that such disclosures awaken suspicion. Why is he making these revelations? Are they a plea for sympathy? Nothing becomes quite so old or odd so quickly as repeated personal revelations. People quickly lose respect for a priest who makes them.

Prayer

If the liturgy is to be prayer and the priest is the leader of the worshiping community, he will need a personal prayer life that is steady, constant, and reliable to remain believable and authentic himself in his own role. Personal prayer must both precede and follow public worship if it is to flow through it. The new liturgy quickly reveals whether a priest is authentically a man of prayer. In the old liturgy, this deficit could be hidden. In the new, it cannot. If it is absent, it now must be disguised through the posturing of prayer, a poor substitute that will easily and quickly be unmasked.

Community

Styles of celebration belong in equal measure to the celebrant and to the worshiping community. They are joint-stock companies, not the personal possession of the celebrant to be carried intact from one community to another. It goes without saying that different communities will call for slightly differing eucharistic celebrations and in turn, different skills from a priest.

There are ethnic and racial differences that mark the celebration of the Eucharist. An African American, Hispanic, Vietnamese, Haitian, or Croatian community will shape the special way in which that community celebrates the Eucharist. For a priest that may call for special language skills. In an upscale suburban community, a seven-to-ten-minute homily is generally about right; in another community, such an offering may be too meager. There are also different groups within suburban parishes. There are special masses for children, teenagers, young adults, engaged and married couples, and the sick. These too call for differing skills on the part of the celebrant. It is a sign of wisdom to know one's limitations. Not everyone is made for the children's mass. Likewise, it is good to know one's strengths, the groups with whom one can most easily speak and celebrate.

The communal side of the equation is often the "given," the side that is more fixed. Worshiping communities have their ways of doing things and they have been encouraged to develop these ways. Other things must revolve around them. Flexibility comes on the side of the celebrant. He must adapt to the ways of the community he enters, not vice versa. It is a bad mistake to misread this situation. However, by adapting to the community, the priest receives his own role as the leader of worship. Over time, he can make an enormous difference.

Chapter Twelve

THE PRIEST AS SHEPHERD

A SHEPHERD WITH A SHEPHERD

P RIESTS ARE SHEPHERDS who have shepherds themselves. In
the case of diocesan priests, they exercise pastoral leadership
under the guidance of a bishop. While priests, especially pastors,
enjoy ample independence, they are accountable to and supported
by a bishop who provides larger vision and oversight for a diocese.
The shepherding office of the local church is spearheaded by priests
and bishop as a team. Therefore the relationship between these
principals is of inestimable importance.

However, it is not always easy to describe. Certainly a psychological template of Freudian caste provides an inadequate measure,
claiming both too little and too much. Priests are simply too variously engaged (or not engaged) with their bishop to make such
generalizations helpful. High-flown theory also tends to overlook
how routine and commonplace the relationship often is.

Priests minister with bishops who are much like themselves.
Priests get used to the ways of the bishop in the same way that
parishioners of a parish who get used to their pastor. In both cases,
patience is a useful virtue. Just as parishioners are long-suffering
with a pastor, so priests generally extend the same courtesy to the
bishop. Some priests may become part of the bishop's inner circle;
one or two, protégés: Priests get to know the bishop's talents and
his vanities. They see clearly that he is a weak and fallible man
much like themselves and are generally accepting of such. Bishops
also are reassigned from time to time. The process of adjusting to
someone else begins anew.

The quality of the relationship between priests and bishop is significant for another reason. Any bishop worth his salt recognizes

that his first duty is to shepherd his priests. They are the ones responsible for the bread-and-butter life of the church, humdrum but essential, that takes place in a parish. Common sense and organizational theory join hands in affirming that no commodity is as scarce or valuable as front-line personnel.

However, the relationship also transcends the pragmatics of common sense. This is the upside that large-scale generalizations may also underestimate. This is a deeply religious relationship. Priests make a formal promise of obedience to their bishop at ordination. He accepts this promise in his own name and in the name of his successors. This exchange colors everything, transforming humdrum life at every point. The bishop's decisions for his priests are part of the working of God's Providence, even when the personal relationship between priest and bishop is difficult. The truth of the proverb that "God writes straight with crooked lines" is nowhere more evident than when such lines pass through the twists and turns of human relationships. For some priests the good opinion and the praise of the bishop are matters of inordinate importance, the blessing of a larger-than-life father figure. (In such cases, psychological interpretations are probably on the money.)

A good bishop encourages the work of every pastor, rendering him a more effective shepherd. By contrast, an inadequate bishop is a burden to a diocese, first borne by priests. But one way or another, the relationship between priests and bishop — personal and religious, humdrum and practical — is vital to the mission of the church. Vatican II underscored the religious character of the bond between priests and bishops. Mutual trust must be the starting point and abiding characteristic of priests' relationships to their bishop.

A GOOD SHEPHERD

Shortly after he was ordained, the bishop made a serious mistake. He became angry at a young priest, berating him in public. As soon as the incident was over, he saw the damage he had done. He vowed, deep inside himself, that he would never do anything like that again. And he didn't. Instead he strove studiously to be courteous in private and public, and after a while it became second nature. If a priest asked a bad or garbled question in public, he would rephrase it into a good one, and then answer it. Recently a priest had exploded at him in a meeting. When the break came, the bishop went over to him and put his hand on his shoulder. "Are you having a bad day, George?" The priest apologized profusely for his discourtesy. When the bishop was moved to a new diocese, he promised himself he would sit down with every priest for half an hour to an hour. It took him a couple of years to do it. He thought to himself, "I can't solve their problems, but at least I can listen to them."

But now with the Charter, he was frankly worried. He personally thought it was unfair to penalize someone for a single incident thirty years ago in an otherwise blameless life, especially in a church that preaches forgiveness. He also thought of the Scripture verse, the way you measure it to others will be measured back to you. But he had also come to some conclusions, at least, for himself. Hard times, he thought, when large issues were uncertain, were the time for small gestures. So of late he had been dropping a note or phoning his priests when he heard good things about them. With so much discouraging news in the media, they deserved a good word. The priests were touched. Even more importantly, they were reassured. An older priest came up to him and said, "Bishop, take care of yourself. You are a good shepherd in tough times."

"The Charter for the Protection of Children and Young People" has a significant wild-card potential for the relationship between priest and bishop. Will it undercut the trust between them? Will it also undercut the bishop's role as a shepherd to his priests? The law of unforeseen consequences is everywhere present.

Yet the law of unforeseen consequences is always balanced by deliberate choice, the bishop's plan of small gestures in hard times. Here the unmistakable challenge of the Charter may itself be a positive factor. If bishops are called to judge priestly conduct more rigorously, they will need to simultaneously balance oversight with increased levels of encouragement and support, consciously given.

The present situation has the potential to pull bishops and priests further apart or bring them together. The best outcome will be the result of deliberate, thoughtful, and courageous action that calls forth untapped reservoirs of generosity and sacrifice. In short, the outcome rests in large measure on the way priests and bishops respond to the challenge.

INTERNAL ATTITUDES

The internal attitudes that a priest brings to the role of shepherd fall into two categories. There are a series of traditional attitudes that belong to a venerable, well-defined religious role that has stayed much the same from one generation to the next. Then there are newer attitudes prompted by the challenge of the era, e.g., newer styles of leadership, the shifting ratio of priests to people, the changing ethnic face of the American church. These make up the special challenge of shepherding at a unique moment in the church's history.

A Pastoral Presence

Essential to the shepherding role in the Catholic tradition is a multiple sense of *presence* that a priest brings to every pastoral task. This flows from the sacrament of Orders and is larger than any one individual or his personal contribution.

A priestly presence is a corporate one. When people knock on the door of a rectory and ask, "Are you the priest?" they tacitly acknowledge how much larger the priestly role is than the individual who stands before them. In effect, each priest carries the corporate weight and reputation of the priesthood, to which he adds his mite. Likewise, it is a public presence even in private moments. In a small town, few actions of the local pastor go unobserved. Invariably, young priests seek out families where they can "be themselves," shedding the weight of a public role. Such arrangements seldom work for long.

A priestly presence is also a powerful one. The priest brings a potent, sacral presence with a unique capacity to heal or harm. The aura of the sacraments surrounds other mundane actions of a priest, making them more potent gestures than he himself may realize. Often, as well, a priest's presence is a political one. Certainly the pope's is. In a diocese in which the church is large and well respected, the bishop is an important public figure who must thread his way through many public controversies. The same can be said of the pastor of a large parish who invariably balances his own constituencies.

Finally, a priest's presence is often a matter of simply *being there.* He shows the flag. He appears for weddings, wakes, picnics, school functions and meetings, often not long. On social occasions, people are just as happy to see him leave as they were to see him come. But he must appear. A priest establishes a sense of pastoral presence by *being there* as expected and announced.

Some priests handle these common public duties more skillfully than others, but the expectations are general. They do, however, raise a crucial question: How well is a heavily symbolic role of a priest joined to the individual personality who bears it? How do public role and personal life go together? Does the public role represent a series of external gestures that are turned on or off at will? Or do public priestly actions carry the natural and easy quality of personal gestures as well? Once again, priests are reminded that not only the liturgy and preaching but newer styles of pastoral leadership reveal a priest's personality at every turn. No one individual ever fits perfectly into such an old and well-defined role as that of a priest. There is always a pinch and sometimes a lingering sense of inadequacy that is best borne with grace and equanimity.

Suffering

The figure of the Good Shepherd in the Gospel of John set the standard for every shepherd in the church. The Good Shepherd knows his sheep by name. He lays down his life for his flock. This is the enduring measure of a shepherd. Priests of Jesus Christ are ordained according to the order of Melchisedek, a new kind of priesthood. They do not kill animals or offer blood sacrifice. If they follow the image of Jesus, they freely offer themselves instead. Christ is both priest and victim who suffers vicariously, offering his life as a ransom for many (Isa. 53). His followers are invited to make up what is lacking in the suffering of Christ. Therefore a willingness to suffer is an essential quality of the priest as shepherd.

Suffering in this sense has become largely an alien virtue. Society can understand suffering in the sense of delayed gratification, e.g., the importance of diet and exercise or moderation in drinking. But this is far different from vicarious suffering on behalf of others whose rationale is uncertain, personal suffering joined to the suffering of Christ as part of a mysterious calculus by which salvation is gained. This rings true only to those with mystical ears. Yet Jesus insists that his followers take up their cross. And their cross should resemble his. While this challenge is there for all Christians, it strikes priests with special force because they aspire, *ex professo,* to be shepherds.

Fidelity to a Lifetime Commitment

This kind of suffering changes names in each age. I think radical discipleship in suffering today takes the form of fidelity to a lifetime commitment made at ordination — at an age too young to understand what it entails — borne over a lifetime. Such perseverance comes only at the price of a sacrifice whose outcome rests mysteriously in the hands of God. Fidelity to a lifetime commitment constitutes an authentic witness to the cross of Christ in today's world.

Such fidelity breaks down into a series of difficult challenges, beginning in the seminary. For idealistic young men in formation, it often takes the form of a desire for a sharp, clear priestly identity in the face of the evident diversity among actual priests. But the priesthood is a corporate charism, and its public face resembles the priests who are presently in the ranks. Consequently its corporate profile may often lack a radical edge. It also incorporates a checkered past that simply cannot be discarded like a snake sheds its skin. Rather, it must be borne by the entire body as an injured limb. History and diversity are a burden and source of suffering for a seminarian who seeks to embrace the radical challenge of a priesthood whose clear edges are sometimes blunted.

The challenge of clear priestly identity, so real for seminarians, disappears with ordination. The priesthood is a social role, and it is learned by interaction with people. When Catholics treat a young man as a priest, he responds accordingly, and the role is imprinted. The process is relatively simple. There are priests one admires and wishes to emulate. There are those whose example one wishes to avoid. Then there is a first assignment, always fateful. The process rolls forward on its own momentum.

Then the challenge changes. It now truly becomes one of perseverance, of lifetime commitment in a society that does not understand, value, or support such commitments, either in marriage or in the priesthood. Long-term commitments that do last seem like anachronisms or happy accidents. The challenge is also shaped by the example of other priests. Diocesan priests these days resemble an aggregate of overworked, underappreciated individual entrepreneurs, whose internal resources are used up far too quickly. Hardly heroic, they resemble journeymen who plug a dike that seems to spring an increasing number of leaks. Nor do priests enter the social arena on a level playing field. A generation or two ago, the field was tipped in their favor, and a priest's flaws were overlooked or forgiven. No longer. Today the field is slightly tilted against them.

In regard to radical commitment, the priesthood is also a child of the time. The task of radicalizing a priestly commitment is placed too much in the hands of each individual priest. For a corporate charism, this seems unfair and unnatural. Although the task of radical commitment must be borne by each priest individually, he must also carry the corporate weight of the priesthood's public reputation. A hard challenge, but heroic virtue appears only in difficult times.

Yet in both good and bad times, the parish priesthood remains a long-term venture. The terms of a pastor's tenure are usually reckoned in six-year increments, not small measures. Stability looms as a high virtue. A priest is expected to be in a parish long enough so that people can join their lives and their families to a certain pastoral vision and to a pastor they respect who invites them to lead better lives. That kind of long-term expectation is met only by a special kind of radical commitment.

Priests realize quickly that half-hearted commitments, even in the short run, are expensive items, often costlier than their radical counterparts. Half-hearted commitments are the children of good intentions and second thoughts and are swept away by the first harsh breeze. Only a radical commitment will stand a sterner test. But most radical commitments are like the kind of adrenalin surge that carries a soldier uphill in the teeth of the enemy, a burst of energy for a single heroic act. What kind of radical commitment meets the test of the long haul?

Radical Commitment for the Long Haul

Since life's actual challenges are seldom fair, sacrifice and suffering are integral to the calculus of a lasting commitment. Any lasting priestly commitment must be able to absorb success and failure, reckoned in personal and professional terms, and come back. Probably more than once.

But first it is important to have hopes, dreams, and aspirations throughout one's entire life. The essence of pastoral leadership is to see the road ahead, to give people a vision of an upland toward which they can strive. The church is precisely that part of the world in which hopes and dreams are unabashedly nourished, in which a piece of the kingdom of God is said to be tangibly present. The essence of shepherding is to give people a sense of higher vision and nobler purpose for their lives.

However, a priest must be able to survive the shipwreck of his hopes and dreams. He has labored for ten years to build up a parish. He leaves and another takes over. In a trice, the work of a decade is seemingly lost, the destruction of one priest's hopes, dreams, and hard work. Bishops probably know the same experience with a diocese. Indeed, all those who have worked diligently in the vineyard of the Lord only to see their work undone by other hands knows this experience. Only with faith can one absorb such defeats and come back for another day. It is easy enough to become embittered and that is everyone's right for a time. But to come back again! That is a special grace of Christ's resurrection in this life.

Long-term radical commitments are also periodically renewed. They are like a number of subcontracts that are constantly being readjusted, renegotiated, and renewed. Probably every seven to ten years a major bridge is crossed. The plain fact is that long-term commitments need to be renewed to stay alive.

There are typical success and failure stories in living such a commitment. The number of mature priests who fall in love at midlife and then honorably leave has probably stayed relatively constant over the years. Likewise, there are priests who have been ill-treated by the church, caught in the maw of a large institution. If lingering bitterness sets the tone of their lives, it makes little difference whether they stay or leave. There are also priests whose inner life has died, but they remain in the priesthood because they lack the courage to leave. Instead they become ecclesiastical functionaries who go through the motions on the dying embers of a once-live commitment. Some are realistic or cynical enough to see that they have neither time, talent, or energy to take up another job, much less another vocation, and so they stay with no virtue at all.

But what of those commitments that truly last, the seed that falls on good soil and flourishes? What do those priests have in common? The first and most obvious quality is that they enjoy being priests and take great personal satisfaction in preaching, celebrating the liturgy, and ministering to people. The emphasis on suffering should not obscure this essential fact. The willingness to suffer helps priests to overcome temporary obstacles, sometimes very large ones. But the chief bearers of continuity in priestly life are personal satisfaction, pride in, and enjoyment of one's vocation. Successful lifelong commitments are those in which priests have been able to surmount obstacles and setbacks in order to renew their own personal satisfaction in being priests. The exercise of priestly ministry according to Vatican II is the chief contributor to priestly holiness. It is also the chief contributor to priestly happiness and satisfaction. These are always major factors in making a lifelong commitment life-giving as well.

Four other qualities come to mind. An education in depth remains a powerful resource to a vigorous priestly commitment. Certainly a spirituality with regular habits of prayer is essential. Then there is sheer grit — the simple force of will, of an interior voice that says, "I will get through this situation, come what may." A stubborn, irrational quality lies at the heart of any lifelong commitment, like the instinct of a camel who knows how to make its way across a bleak stretch of desert. An abiding confidence in God's Providence is paramount as well, faith in a kindly light that leads us more surely and safely than our own instincts ever could.

It is often said that the challenge of the age to the priesthood is celibacy. An equal argument can be made that the real but less apparent challenge is the challenge of a lifetime commitment, lived with abiding vigor. In an age of great change, what is more valuable than the permanent commitment of individuals? Such commitments are stanchions of a bridge across which people walk as they seek to pass down their faith to their children.

Collegiality and Collaboration

Collegiality and collaboration, new attitudes essential for shepherding today, stretch across the distinction between internal attitude and practical skills, belonging in full measure on both sides of the ledger.

The attitude was born at Vatican II, springing from a simple but revolutionary insight. If the bishops were co-responsible with the pope for the church universal at an ecumenical council, do they not bear a similar responsibility under ordinary circumstances too? Hence was born the notion of the collegial responsibility of the bishops with the pope for the welfare of the church universal and of their collaboration effort in discharging this duty. These two ideas quickly became trickle-down insights that caught on at the grassroots level, transforming pastoral ministry in the Catholic Church in every way. A veritable floodgate was opened. For if the bishops were co responsible with the pope for the church as a whole, then were not priests co-responsible with the bishop for the local church? By the same token, were not the people of a parish co-responsible with their pastor for the welfare of the parish?

If the appearance of collegiality and collaboration was dramatic and sudden, their birth in the first generation was not always easy. In the United States, the overlap of these ideas with egalitarian impulses and democratic practices was natural. The first result of the mix was mild organizational turmoil in which various levels of decision-making were sometimes confused. The truth was that collaborative relationships were complex, not simple, and the only available models from democratic processes were satisfactory and unsatisfactory in equal measure.

THE CHAIRS

St. Michael the Archangel parish bought one hundred portable chairs in 1967. Very good portable chairs. They lent them out for civic functions and to other churches. The decision to do so was made by the pastor after talking to the janitor.

After the council, the pastor organized a parish committee and pledged to share authority with its elected members. They were jointly responsible for the welfare of the parish, he told them. At a subsequent meeting, a request came from the Presbyterian church to borrow the chairs. There had been bad blood between Catholics and Presbyterians in this town for generations. When the pastor brought the request to the parish council with his own positive recommendation, he was voted down, ten to two. No chairs for Presbyterians around here. The pastor was mortified by the decision and visited the Presbyterian minister to convey the news in person. He explained that Catholics were implementing collegial leadership and he had lost the vote. The minister smiled at him wryly and said, "Welcome to the club."

After the implementation of the 1983 Code of Canon Law, the "pastoral council" replaced the parish committee. Canonically, it possessed a consultative voice. The next year another request for the chairs came from the Presbyterian church. The pastor consulted his parish council and carefully explained that a new era was dawning that called for new gestures. He had carefully sounded out each member and took a consultative vote. This time the vote was unanimous in his favor. The Presbyterians finally got the chairs.

Clearly collaborative relationships are complex. There is decision-making authority. Who signs the checkbook or, in this case, who makes the final decision on the chairs? Then there is moral authority; a bishop's and a pastor's real authority is moral. There are also consultative relationships and a more amorphous yet no less real feeling of co-responsibility. Not surprisingly, the maiden voyage of collegiality and collaboration in the Catholic Church often took the form of a cruise in choppy waters.

Collaborative ministry in the first generation, while often exciting, also carried a fair measure of frustration. It often seemed as if the Holy Spirit had hovered over the church and given birth to a glass egg of middle management: meetings, minutes, reports (usually unread), committees, subcommittees, and task forces. It was like the old saying, the mountains roar and out comes a mouse. In effect, the human input was disproportionately high compared to the real output at the end of the day.

The seemingly simple and user-friendly ideas of collegiality and collaboration became in practice something closer to learning to ride a unicycle. Balance is everything, and balance is learned only slowly. But a generation later, the ride has become smoother. Grassroot outcomes are the most impressive. Increasingly, parishioners feel co-responsible with the pastor for the welfare of the parish. In many parishes church attendance was not markedly affected by the sexual abuse scandals. It is a fair surmise to attribute this in some measure to the fruits of collegiality and collaboration in their second generation. Catholic parishioners often have a high sense of ownership of their parish and its welfare. It is fortuitous that this development occurs at a time when the ratio of the numbers of priests to people in the American church is changing. Increasingly lay women and men will be asked to assume greater responsibilities in their parish and in their diocese.

This development surely calls for new attitudes toward shepherding on the part of priests. The internal attitude of priests toward lay participation and responsibility cannot be grudging. Since the parish belongs collegially to the people of the parish, with the priest as their shepherd, his shepherding role at its most essential points is carried out collaboratively with his parishioners. They are responsible together for assuring that the marks of the church — one, holy, catholic, and apostolic — shine forth brightly.

PRACTICAL SKILLS

The Current Situation

The practical skills for shepherding these days must be firmly located against the background of the revolution in pastoral ministry
that has occurred in the past two generations. An active Catholic
parish in the 1950s in the United States usually devoted its energy and resources to operating a Catholic grade school and high
school with a few auxiliary organizations: the Legion of Mary, the
St. Vincent de Paul Society, the Knights of Columbus. Now in many
parishes, the commitment to schools has been replaced or eclipsed
by a vast cornucopia of ministries that address the diverse needs of
parishioners. The spread of activities is amazing.

A MINISTRIES FAIR

*A parish of about two thousand families on the central coast of
California sponsored a ministries fair on Sunday, June 8, 2003. The
purpose of the fair was to acquaint parishioners with the activi-
ties of the parish and seek new volunteers for its programs. They
include: RCIA (Rite of Christian Initiation for Adults), Vacation
Bible School, Confirmation — Sophomores through Seniors, First
Eucharist Program, Lambs for Jesus, Children's Liturgy of the Word,
Faith in the Home, Religious Education, Pre-Marriage Preparation,
Pre-Baptismal Preparation, Small Christian Communities, Focus,
Lifeteen, Refocus/Marriage Enrichment, RCIC (Rite of Christian
Initiation for Children), Bible Study, Divorced/Separated Catholics,
Eucharistic Ministers, Lay Presiders, Music, Perpetual Adoration,
Greeters, Sacristans, Lectors, Ushers, Grief Bereavement Support,
Ministry with People with Disabilities, Young Family Socials, Parish
Newsletter, Prayer Tree, Satellite Shelter, Transportation, Giving
Tree, Ministry to the Elderly, Prison Ministry, St. Vincent de Paul
Society, Knights of Columbus, ICF (Italian Catholic Federation),
Golf Tournament, Social Committee, Martha's Pantry, Gatherings
for Parishioners, Funeral Reception, Stewardship, Bulletin Board,
Commission of Ministries, Office Assistants, Co-sponsored Parish*

Schools (Good Shepherd Grade School, St. Francis Diocesan High School).

The parish has a single full-time priest. What does it mean to be the pastor of such a parish?

The parish described here is only one kind of parish. The challenge is different but equally complex in a parish serving diverse ethnic groups, Latinos, Vietnamese, and Filipinos, for example, mixed with an older Anglo component who perhaps founded the parish and built the church. In effect, the pastor is running three or four parishes under one roof. Here the most influential group may be the "Space Committee," which decides on questions of space and time. Who gets to use the church or parish hall and when?

Long-term ventures have been a hallmark of the Catholic Church in the modern era. In regard to both the interpretation of the Scriptures and Catholic social teaching, steady development over more than a hundred years has paid enormous dividends in consistent but flexible approaches. In this case, however, the cutting edge of collaborative ministry as a long-term venture is not located at central services or in theological schools. The front line is the local parish. The lead agent is the local pastor.

A long-haul venture calls for long-haul skills. The need for action, decisions, and presence could quickly eat up the energy of a single priest, even a team of priests. If the past generation has taught us anything, it is about the need for *thoughtful, deliberate* action so that old mistakes are not repeated. Thoughtful, deliberate pastoral activity seems to be the precondition for church law and theology to do their respective tasks, further clarifying complex relationships and reflecting on the theological import of pastoral activity.

Five Practical Skills

First, professional standards. There are obvious management skills required to run a large parish staff and special skills needed for directing volunteers. Regular staff meetings, clear lines of accountability, and performance reviews have become standard. One need not be a lawyer or accountant to read a balance sheet or know when

legal advice is needed. Then there is the question of personal conduct in professional situations, and here the pastor sets the tone.
This issue is especially important for priests at this moment. Rule
one should be that all situations with parishioners must be regarded
as professional ones; a clear sense of personal and professional limits should be everywhere evident. In doubtful situations, one should
err on the side of caution.

Second, the ability to work collaboratively with women. Theology and common sense unite on this issue. Pope John Paul II has
declared that in regard to the ordination of women, the church's
hands are tied. According to *Ordinatio Sacerdotalis* (1994), the position is definitive, belonging to the secondary object of infallibility.
But in order to avoid the impression of discrimination, the church
at the same time on every level has made countless statements
about the value, dignity, and importance of women in society and
in the church. If Catholic women take these statements to the bank
of experience to find they are not redeemable in the genuine coin of
the realm, the church is in major trouble. An old pastor puts his finger on the reason. For a single event, a parish bazaar, for example,
the men of the parish are dependable. But the steady, consistent
volunteer work of the parish is carried out by the women. The natural fact of two generations ago has found current expression in
programs for lay ecclesial formation. The number of lay ministers
in formation tripled from 10,500 in 1985 to 35,448 in 2003. Sixty
percent of those enrolled in such formation programs are women.[1]

Yet the issue goes beyond pragmatics. The movement for the
equality and dignity of women in society represents a significant
moral force in its own right. The church would not be true to itself
if it did not recognize, embrace and reflect this movement in its
own life.

Third, the ability to work effectively with small groups. One-to-
one counseling, while it still takes place, is increasingly relegated
to professionals. A priest's most effective work takes place with
small groups, and guiding small groups is a special skill that can be
learned but cannot be assumed. An inadequate grasp of small group
dynamics is a serious hindrance to pastoral effectiveness these days.
The faults here are common enough. The pastor may dominate the

discussion or, at the other end, he may abdicate authority, allowing vocal members to dominate. The great virtues are moderation, balance, and patience. A wise pastor also makes sure that the turnover of membership on major committees is gradual. This insures that a corporate memory remains, enabling the group to undertake long-term projects and avoid old mistakes.

Fourth, a capacity for articulate speech. A good pastor who is a poor homilist can always manage. Over time, as people get to know him, they overlook his lack of skill in the pulpit. But the default position should not obscure the enormous boon that good preaching brings to pastoral leadership. Beyond preaching, the ability to explain the goals of the parish in an effective way is an enormously effective pastoral skill. Moral authority depends on the art of persuasion. Persuasion depends on a gift for articulate speech in the pulpit, in parish committees, and with the staff. A shepherd who can articulate his vision in a compelling way is more than halfway home.

Fifth, emotional intelligence. The phrase belongs to Daniel Goleman.[2] Emotional intelligence is native to some but it also can be learned. Men seem to have more difficulty with this skill than women. It means being able to bring one's own feelings to articulate speech. It means as well the ability to interpret the emotional, as distinct from the intellectual, content of what others say. At a minimum, it means not being stampeded into a hasty reaction by the strong emotional outbursts of people under stress. How does one hold people accountable and at times deliver a reprimand in a respectful way? How does one fire a person or terminate a contract in a courteous manner, without a hint of anger? How does one absorb the negative reaction of others in such situations and not return the same in kind? These are vitally important pastoral skills.

A final thought. A good shepherd these days is a good listener. There was an old saying that elevation to the episcopate brought a darkening of the intellect and a strengthening of the will. The same phenomenon probably occurs at every step on the ascending ladder of authority. It is also an ecumenical and, indeed a secular phenomenon as well. That means that the judgment of one's own ability to listen is always a matter of perspective. The bishop *thinks* he listens to the priests. The priests think the bishop does what he wants. Getting the bishop to listen to other voices, especially opposing ones, means assembling a *force majeure*. Most parish councils would say the same of the pastor. He, too, *thinks* he listens. The simple act of genuine listening is an enduring challenge because the brunt of leadership is to move a large venture forward. In doing so, certain voices must necessarily be overlooked or discounted. But is the choice the right one? No simple answer can be given. In fact, no simple prepackaged formula can capture the role of an effective pastor. In the last analysis, it is the actual challenge itself that makes the shepherd, and today's challenge is large.

EPILOGUE

I HAVE NOTED that newer styles of preaching, presiding, and pastoral leadership reveal more about a priest's personality than he realizes. How true is the same point about a book on spirituality and priestly formation? How much does an author so given to the use of vignettes tip his own hand in the process? How much is objective analysis and how much the memoir of a single priest? I will let it to the readers to answer those questions. I close with some thoughts on why I began this book and on my own hopes and fears as I conclude it.

I wrote this book because I care deeply about the Roman Catholic priesthood. Like other Catholics, I was horrified at and scandalized by the steady stream of stories of the sexual abuse of children and young people by priests that began rolling out in January 2002. I was revolted by attempts to hide these incidents, ignore victims and evade responsibility. For me as a priest, horror mixed with shame because I could not separate myself from the perpetrators of such unspeakable deeds. I was joined to them in the priesthood of Jesus Christ. My dismay only grew as I realized that evil deeds done long ago could now be creating new victims, other priests who may be falsely accused or quickly judged. Evil deeds continue to beget their own kind. Like many bad gifts from the past, they have not ceased giving.

At the same time, I was struck afresh by René Girard's thought that the spirit that raised Jesus from the dead was something new that this world could not produce on its own, a spirit of courage without violence, of courage now mixed with forgiveness. Jesus's followers never sought to revenge his death. The dying Jesus in Luke's Gospel gives his disciples the lesson: "Father, forgive them; for they do not know what they are doing" (Luke 23:34).

In the same spirit I began this book. I have tried not to apportion blame anew to participants in these events — more to bishops, less to priests, more to the past, less to the present. There is blame enough to go around and everyone's cup is filled. Instead, I have tried to say something positive about the priesthood in order to rekindle in priests the highest ideals of their vocation. The hope is to call forth a heroic response at a difficult moment. The tableau about the good shepherd (pp. 195–96 above) says much about me. In hard times, when many large issues hang in suspension, what is the one positive thing I can do? For me it was to write this book with as little recrimination and rancor as possible in a sea awash with those sentiments. In hard times, this is my own small offering.

My hope is that in time, as the scandals begin to recede, the bishops will convene a new plenary council of Baltimore. But in this age, although a meeting of bishops might be a necessary first step, a truly serious meeting would include some representation of priests, deacons, religious, and laity. It would be peculiar if the laity were not included, as if they are invited to oversee the most troubling issue facing the church — sexual abuse by priests and complicity by bishops — but are excluded from plans to chart the future.

This is not to introduce the principle of representative democracy into a hierarchical church. Something different is at stake here. The issue is about unity and diversity in a very active church in which collaboration has been encouraged for two generations. What we seek in our church, which is often as fractious as the society in which we live, is a unity in the midst of our diversity and a center — as broad-based as possible — that will hold. This is a worthy goal for a faith that adores one God in three persons.

This much is crystal clear. We need a large public gesture of a positive nature to pull us into the future. We need it as much for ourselves as for others. To repeat Lukacs's distinction, we have motive enough right now to go forward, the push from the past, the bruising experience of the scandals. What we need is the pull of the future, a new sense of purpose. We are a large community and need a corresponding communal gesture. But a council is not a panacea and not without risk. On the contrary, it represents a big gamble, if only by way of raising false hopes. But what is the alternative? To languish indefinitely in the shadow of past mistakes. My hope for such a council developed after I began this book. But at the end, it stands as one man's hope.

My fear is that in response to the scandals in my own generation, younger priests will turn to an older template of the priesthood by way of reaction. If in the process they become protective of priestly prerogatives and resentful of lay collaboration, I fear a train wreck down the line. To see a clash on this front between young priests, who are few in number, and active laity, who are already on the job in large numbers, would be a needless tragedy and a false reading of lay aspiration. Laity involved in church ministry say with one voice that they need good priests to make their own ministry effective.

The truth here is that the theology of priesthood that emerged from Vatican II in the first generation was perhaps not lofty enough to call for heroic sacrifice or to justify the cost of the discipline of celibacy. On this point young priests may be right in their instincts. But an elevated theology of priesthood will not be found in a return to the theology of the past or by assembling the surface accouterments of an older era, e.g., birettas, amices, and palls. Such gestures speak only of human need, fear, and uncertainty. Such emotions are understandable, but they are not positive enough to chart a course into the future. A loftier theology of the priesthood may yet lie ahead. But it must come on its own as a genuine movement of the spirit. Still, we will be spared no human travail when it arrives.

The transition between generations in any vocation is always perilous. Each generation imagines the future as the realization of the dreams it had in its youth. In reality, the ideals of one generation are replaced by those of another, which the older generation never fully understands or accepts. Given this natural disjunction, the transition from an older generation in the priesthood to my own after Vatican II was far too abrupt. To follow one abrupt transition with another is not good. Yet one fact remains. The shift of generations will be fought out in small gestures at the liturgy. For Catholics, it always is. These are power-moves, no surprise for a theology of priesthood, still on the books, that centered on the power to consecrate and the power to forgive sins. It remains part of the equation.

We now carry the legacy of Vatican II into its third generation. At the beginning of the journey, we often spoke about a pilgrim people and the phrase carried an upbeat note. Now we sometimes resemble weary travelers on the high sea without land in sight, the children of Israel murmuring in the desert, pining for the fleshpots of Egypt, which they were happy to leave a scant generation ago. But the task of carrying forward the reforms of a great council remains a bracing challenge, broad enough to span generations, joining them together in a sense of common purpose. Is this not what we seek and need at the present moment?

In our own vision of God — Father, Son, and Spirit — a primordial change of generations stands enshrined. From the Father to the Son in the Spirit. "In the Divinity, Father and Son unfold the quality of being, by spreading it through two generations. And the Spirit, lest he be confused with the wit of the moment, is explicitly said to descend from the interaction of two generations, the Father and the Son."[1] Surely the divine pathos by which the Father sends the Son stands over and blesses all who in later generations undertake perilous journeys in the Son's name.

NOTES

Introduction

1. John Lukacs, *At the End of an Age* (New Haven: Yale University Press, 2002). Lukas counts the twentieth as a "short century, lasting from 1914 to 1989, seventy-five years" (29).

2. Daniel Lyons, "Sex, God, and Greed," *Forbes* 171, no. 12 (June 9, 2003): 66–72.

3. A Gallup pole indicated that by year's end 2002, Catholic church attendance had declined by 7 percentage points since the previous March. Cited in Peter Steinfels, *A People Adrift* (New York: Simon & Schuster, 2003), 41.

4. Pope John Paul II, *Novo Millennio Ineunte,* 1.

5. Pope John Paul II, *Crossing the Threshold of Hope,* ed. Vittorio Messori (New York: Alfred A. Knopf, 1994), 4–14.

6. Lukacs, *At the End of an Age,* 60.

Chapter One: The Scandals

1. Clifford Geertz, *The Interpretation of Culture* (New York: Basic Books, 1973), 3–30. "Thick description" is a term coined by anthropologist Clifford Geertz to describe the layered, rich, and contextual description of an event or social scene.

2. Avishai Margalit, *The Ethics of Memory* (Cambridge: Harvard University Press, 2002), 1–17

3. Henricus Denzinger and Adolfus Schönmetzer, S.J., eds., *Enchiridion Symbolorum* (Freiburg im Bresgau: Herder, 1965), 1763–78.

4. Reiner Kaczynski, "Toward the Reform of the Liturgy," in *History of Vatican II,* vol. 3, ed. Giuseppe Alberigo, English edition by Joseph A. Komonchak (Maryknoll, N.Y.: Orbis and Leuven: Peeters, 2000), 231.

5. Eamon Duffy, *Saints and Sinners: A History of the Pope* (New Haven: Yale Nota Bene, 2001), 323.

6. Kaczynski, "Toward the Reform of the Liturgy," 219.

7. Quoted in a eulogy by Dr. Thomas A. Drolesky in the *Catholic Voice* newsletter of the Society of Traditional Roman Catholics (Mead, Wash.) 18, no. 4 (December 2002): 1.

8. Ludwig Ott, *Fundamentals of Catholic Dogma*, trans. Patrick Lynch, English edition edited by James Canon Bastible, D.D. (Rockford Ill.: Tan Books and Publishers, 1974), 433.

9. *Code of Canon Law, Latin-English Edition*, trans. under the auspices of the Canon Law Society of America (Washington, D.C.: Canon Law Society of America, 1983), 357–62.

10. Charles R. Morris, *American Catholic* (New York: Times Books, 1997), 361–62.

11. Morris McGregor, "O'Boyle, Patrick Aloysius (1896–1987)," in *The Encyclopedia of American Catholic History*, ed. Michael Glazier and Thomas J. Shelley (Collegeville, Minn.: Liturgical Press, 1997), 1064–66.

12. Quoted in Joyce Milton, *The Road to Malpsychia* (San Francisco: Encounter Books, 2002), 139–40.

13. Anita M. Caspary, *Witness to Integrity* (Collegeville, Minn.: Liturgical Press, 2003). Caspary presents a broad, sympathetic portrait. She also disagrees with Coulson and Milton on the negative impact of humanistic psychology, 239–41.

14. Milton, *The Road to Malpsychia*, 235.

15. Ibid., 145.

16. St. Mary's Faculty Minutes, 1791–1886, Archives of the U.S. Province of the Society of St. Sulpice.

17. Mary L. Gauthier, *Catholic Ministry Formation Directory: 2003*, Center for Applied Research in the Apostolate (CARA) (Washington, D.C.: Georgetown University, 2003), 2.

18. Laurie Goodstein, "Decades of Damage: Trail of Pain in Church Crisis Leads to Nearly Every Diocese," *New York Times*, January 12, 2003, 21, statistics from *Annuarium Statisticum Ecclesiae*, Rome: Libreria Editrice Vaticana.

19. What Morris stated remains true (Morris, *American Catholic*, 379). There are no reliable statistics on the number of homosexual priests or seminarians, then or now, i.e., there are no statistics based on random samples, only self-selected ones, and no way of knowing how representative they are. The same is true of statistics culled from individual clinical practice.

20. Duffy, *Saints and Sinners*, 369.

21. Goodstein, "Decades of Damage," 1, 20–21.

22. Ibid., 1.

23. Ibid., 21.

24. Ibid., 20.

25. Ibid.

26. *The Program of Priestly Formation* (Washington, D.C.: NCCB, 1993).

Chapter Two: *This Generation of Seminarians, This Generation of Seminaries*

1. *Optatam Totius,* Decree on the Training of Priests, *Vatican Council II, The Conciliar and Post Conciliar Documents,* Austin Flannery, O.P., general editor (Northport, N.Y.: Costello Publishing Company, 1980), 1.

2. Mary L. Gauthier, *Catholic Ministry Formation Directory: 2003,* Center for Applied Research in the Apostolate (CARA) (Washington, D.C.: Georgetown University, 2003), 1–2.

3. Ibid., 2. There were 29,224 seminarians in high school and college in 1967/1968 compared to 2,184 in 2002/2003.

4. Ibid.

5. Ibid., "Frequently Requested Church Statistics," 2003, 1.

6. Hans Urs Von Balthasar, *Theo-drama,* vol. 3: *Dramatis Personae: Persons in Christ,* trans. Graham Harrison (San Francisco: Ignatius Press, 1992), 297.

7. On age and ethnic composition of current seminarians, see Gauthier, *Catholic Ministry Formation Directory: 2003,* 1–2. 2003, 11.

8. Remark of a Lutheran pastor to Father Frank Norris, S.S., translator for Protestant and Orthodox observers at Vatican II.

Chapter Three: *The Evangelical Counsels*

1. *Lumen Gentium,* Dogmatic Constitution on the Church, 43.

2. Adolphe Tanquerey, S.S., *The Spiritual Life: A Treatise on Ascetical and Mystical Theology,* trans. Herman Branderis (Tournai: Desclée, 1930).

Chapter Four: *Prayer*

1. *Sacrosanctum Concilium,* Constitution on the Sacred Liturgy, 14.

2. Hans Urs Von Balthasar, *Glory of the Lord,* vol. 1: *Seeing the Form,* trans. Erasmo Leiva-Merikakis (San Francisco: Ignatius, 1982), 220, 251.

3. François Fenelon, *Letters to Men and Women,* ed. Standford Derek, trans. H. L. Sidney Lear (Westminster, Md.: Newman Press, 1957), 127.

4. Ernst Käsemann, *Jesus Means Freedom,* trans. Charles Frank (Philadelphia: Fortress Press, 1968), 39.

5. "The General Instruction of the Liturgy of the Hours," *The Liturgy of the Hours,* 4 vols. (New York: Catholic Publishing, 1975), 1:21–98.

6. See n. 4 above.

7. William James, *The Varieties of Religious Experience* (New York: Mentor Books, 1958), 54.

Chapter Five: The Challenge of Simplicity of Life

1. William James, *The Principles of Psychology* (New York: Dover Publications, 1950), 1:291.

2. Søren Kierkegaard, *Concluding Unscientific Postscript*, ed. Walter Lowrie, trans. David F. Swenson (Princeton, N.J.: Princeton University Press, 1968), 55.

3. Søren Kierkegaard, *Christian Discourses*, trans. Walter Lowrie (Oxford: Oxford University Press, 1940), 76.

4. John Henry Newman, *Parochial and Plain Sermons* (San Francisco: Ignatius Press, 1997), 31–40.

Chapter Six: The Challenge of Celibacy

1. Elizabeth Hayt, "It's Never Too Late to Be a Virgin," *New York Times*, August 4, 2002, section 9, 1.

2. Margaret Talbot, "When Men Taunt Men, Is It Sexual Harassment?" *New York Times Magazine*, October 13, 2002, 55.

3. Raymond E. Brown, S.S., *An Introduction to the New Testament* (New York: Doubleday, 1996), 194.

4. Ibid., 321–22.

Chapter Seven: The Challenge of Authority and Obedience

1. G. K. Chesterton, *Orthodoxy* (New York: Doubleday, 1990), 81–101.

2. Eamon Duffy, *Saints and Sinners: A History of the Pope* (New Haven: Yale Nota Bene, 2001), 387–95.

3. Hans Urs Von Balthasar, *Glory of the Lord*, vol. 1, *Seeing the Form*, trans. Erasmo Leiva-Merikakis (San Francisco: Ignatius, 1982), 229.

4. Ralph Waldo Emerson, *Essays and Lectures* (New York: Library of America, 1983), 495.

5. Ibid.

6. *Presbyterorum Ordinis*, 15.

7. G. K. Chesterton, *Heretics* (Salem, N.H.: Ayer, 1970), 67.

Chapter Eight: The Doctrine of the Priesthood

1. John Henry Newman, *An Essay on the Development of Christian Doctrine* (Garden City, N.Y.: Image Books, 1960), 177–83.

2. Henricus Denzinger and Adolfus Schönmetzer, S.J., eds. *Enchiridion Symbolorum* (Freiburg im Bresgau: Herder, 1965), 1716–19.

3. Bernard Lonergan, *Method in Theology* (New York: Herder and Herder, 1972), 295–353.

4. Kenan Osborne, O.F.M., *Priesthood: A History of Ordained Ministry in the Roman Catholic Church* (New York: Paulist Press, 1988), 215.

5. Denzinger and Schönmetzer, *Enchiridion,* 1326.

6. Ibid., 1763–78.

7. *The Roman Catechism: The Catechism of the Council of Trent* (Rockford, Ill.: Tan Books and Publisher, 1982), 317–37.

8. Ibid., 318.

9. Ibid., 329.

10. Ibid., 332–34.

11. Osborne, *Priesthood,* 281.

12. Denzinger and Schönmetzer, *Enchiridion,* 3857–61.

13. Ludwig Ott, *Fundamentals of Catholic Dogma,* trans. Patrick Lynch, English edition edited by James Canon Bastible, D.D. (Rockford Ill.: Tan Books and Publishers, 1974), 452–53.

14. Osborne, *Priesthood,* 261.

15. *Lumen Gentium,* 5.

16. Ibid., 10.

17. Ibid., 31.

18. *Presbyterorum Ordinis,* Decree on the Ministry and Life of Priest, 4.

19. *Sacrosanctum Concilium,* 56.

20. *Lumen Gentium,* 25.

21. Ibid., 21.

22. Ibid., 28, 29.

23. *Catechism of the Catholic Church* (New York: Doubleday, 1997), nos. 1537–1600, 427–46.

24. Karl Rahner, "Toward a Fundamental Theological Interpretation of Vatican II," *Theological Studies* 40, no. 4 (1979): 716–27; also in *Theological Investigations* 20, trans. Edward Quinn (New York: Crossroad, 1981), 77–89.

25. Eugen Rosenstock-Heussy, *Out of Revolution* (Norwich, Vt.: Argo Books, 1969), 135, 137, 260f., 349–52, 364, 701f.

26. Ibid., 134.

27. Ernst Käsemann, *Jesus Means Freedom,* trans. Charles Frank (Philadelphia: Fortress Press, 1968), 87.

28. John Tracy Ellis, "The Formation of the American Priest: An Historical Perspective," in *The Catholic Priest in the United States*, ed. John Tracy Ellis (Collegeville, Minn.: Saint John's University Press, 1971), 44–50.

Chapter Nine: The Theology of the Priesthood

1. Han Urs Von Balthasar, *Theo-drama*, vol. 3: *Dramatis Personae: Persons in Christ*, trans. Graham Harrison (San Francisco: Ignatius Press, 1992), 25–32.

2. Blaise Pascal, *Pensées*, trans. A. J. Krailsheimer. (London: Penguin Books, 1995), 905.

3. Karl Rahner, S.J., *On the Theology of Death*, trans. Charles H. Henkey (New York: Herder and Herder, 1962), 71.

4. Réne Girard, *I See Satan Fall Like Lightning*, trans. James G. Williams (Maryknoll, N.Y.: Orbis Books, 2002), 137–60.

5. John Henry Newman, *An Essay on the Development of Christian Doctrine* (Garden City, N.Y.: Image Books, 1960), 95–108.

6. *Sacrosanctum Concilium*, 7.

7. Ibid.

8. Avishai Margalit, *The Ethics of Memory* (Cambridge: Harvard University Press, 2002), 13.

9. Johann Adam Moehler, *Unity in the Church, or, the Principle of Catholicism*, trans. Peter C. Erg (Washington, D.C.: Catholic University of America Press, 1996).

10. *Catechism of the Catholic Church* (New York: Doubleday, 1997), 811.

11. Henricus Denzinger and Adolfus Schönmetzer, S.J., eds. *Enchiridion Symbolorum* (Freiburg im Bresgau: Herder, 1965), 3014.

12. Pascal, *Pensées*, 604.

13. John Henry Newman, *Parochial and Plain Sermons* (San Francisco: Ignatius Press, 1997), 1648–55.

14. Ibid., 1654.

15. *The Rites of the Catholic Church* (Collegeville, Minn.: A Pueblo Book/Liturgical Press, 1991), 2:46.

Chapter Ten: The Priest as Minister of the Word

1. *Presbyterorum Ordinis*, 12.

2. Ibid., 4.

3. Joseph Lash, *Helen and Teacher: The Story of Helen Keller and Anne Sullivan* (New York: Delacorte Press, 1980), 55.

4. Eugen Rosenstock-Heussy, *Practical Knowledge of the Soul* (Norwich, Vt.: Argo Books, 1988), 27.

5. Carl Bernstein and Marco Politi, *His Holiness* (New York: Doubleday, 1996), 377.

6. George Weigel, *Witness to Hope* (New York: Cliff Street Books, 1999), 462.

7. Ibid., 546–47.

8. Ibid., 812.

9. G. K. Chesterton, *Orthodoxy* (New York: Doubleday, 1990), 22.

10. Pontifical Biblical Commission, *The Interpretation of the Bible in the Church* (Boston: St. Paul Books & Media, 1993), 75.

11. Ernst Käsemann, *Jesus Means Freedom*, trans. Charles Frank (Philadelphia: Fortress Press, 1968), 71.

Chapter Eleven: The Priest as Minister of the Sacrament

1. Henricus Denzinger and Adolfus Schönmetzer, S.J., eds. *Enchiridion Symbolorum* (Freiburg im Bresgau: Herder, 1965), 1608.

2. Iris Murdoch, *The Bell* (New York: Penguin Books, 2001), 289–90.

3. Robert Sokolowski, *Eucharistic Presence: A Study in the Theology of Disclosure* (Washington, D.C.: Catholic University of America Press, 1993), 13–21.

Chapter Twelve: The Priest as Shepherd

1. Mary L. Gauthier, *Catholic Ministry Formation Directory: 2003*, Center for Applied Research in the Apostolate (CARA) (Washington, D.C.: Georgetown University, 2003), 188–90.

2. Daniel Goleman, *Emotional Intelligence* (New York: Bantam Books, 1995).

Epilogue

1. Eugen Rosenstock-Heussy, *The Christian Future or the Modern Mind Outrun* (New York: Charles Scribner's Sons, 1946), 219–20.

ABOUT THE AUTHOR

Howard P. Bleichner, S.S., a systematic theologian at St. Patrick's Seminary in Menlo Park, California, is a leading figure in American priestly formation. For one decade he served as President and Rector of St. Patrick's Seminary in San Francisco, and for another decade as Rector of the Theological College of the Catholic University of America. He was editor of volumes 1 and 2 of the *Norms for Priestly Formation*, and editor of the fourth edition of *The Program of Priestly Formation*. Fr. Bleichner holds a B.A. from Dartmouth College and a D.Theol. from the Catholic Faculty of the University of Tuebingen (magna cum laude).

Of Related Interest

Mark S. Massa, S.J.
ANTI-CATHOLICISM IN AMERICA
The Last Acceptable Prejudice

One of the most important books in religion in recent years, this is a tour de force of new investigation, scholarly rigor, storytelling, and humor. In this authoritative work, Mark Massa, program director of Fordham University's Center for American Catholic Studies, reveals how American Catholics' distinctive way of viewing the world is constantly misunderstood — and attacked — by outsiders. From controversy surrounding political candidates, intellectuals, artists, and personalities in the media to figures in religion and science, this book tells the astonishing story of how a supposedly tolerant American culture has mistreated and prejudged members of its largest religious group.

0-8245-2129-3, $24.95 hardcover

Mark Massa, S.J.
CATHOLICS AND AMERICAN CULTURE
Fulton Sheen, Dorothy Day, and the Notre Dame Football Team

While in the early years of the twentieth century Catholics in America were for the most part distrusted outsiders with respect to the dominant culture, by the 1960s the mainstream of American Catholicism was in many ways "the culture's loudest and most uncritical cheerleader." Mark Massa explores the rich irony in this postwar transition, beginning with the heresy case of Leonard Feeney, examining key figures such as Fulton Sheen, Thomas Merton, and John F. Kennedy, and concluding with a look at the University of Notre Dame and the transformed status of American Catholic higher education.

0-8245-1955-8, $19.95 paperback

crossroad

Of Related Interest

Deal Hudson
An American Conversion
One Man's Discovery of Beauty and Truth
in Times of Crisis

Crisis magazine publisher, syndicated radio host, and frequent guest on national media, Hudson offers his memoir of the beauty and truth of the Catholic faith as seen through the eyes of one of today's most prominent converts.

0-8245-2126-9, $22.95 hardcover